Shostakovich: Socialism, Stalin & Symphonies

Shostakovich:
Socialism, Stalin & Symphonies

by Simon Behrman

Revolutionary Portrait: 9

Shostakovich: Socialism, Stalin & Symphonies
by Simon Behrman
Published June 2010
by Redwords
1 Bloomsbury Street, London WC1B 3QE

www.redwords.org.uk

ISBN: 9781905192663

Design and production: Roger Huddle
Set in Sabon and Univers

Printed by MPG Biddles Limited, Norfolk PE30 4LS

© Simon Behrman

Redwords is linked to Bookmarks the Socialist Bookshop
www.bookmarksbookshop.co.uk

About the author:
Simon Behrman writes regularly on classical music and other
subjects for *Socialist Worker*, *Socialist Review* and *International
Socialism Journal*. He lives in east London, and is currently
researching for a PhD in law at Birkbeck College.

Contents

Acknowledgements **8**

Introduction **9**

1: Classical music and revolution **15**

2: Child of the revolution **21**

3: The Golden Age **31**

4: Composing a revolution **39**

5: The end of the party **53**

6: Terror and resistance **63**

7: From war hero to pariah **73**

8: The Thaw **85**

9: Decay **99**

Epilogue: 'The Shostakovich Wars' **105**

Notes to text **109**

Further reading **115**

Further listening **117**

Acknowledgements

My thanks go first to Roger Huddle for encouraging me to write this book in the first place. Jesse Oldershaw helped with accessing books (and paid the library fines!). Louis Bayman, Bernard Behrman, Terri Behrman, Jess Edwards and Someye Zadeh all read the book in draft and provided me with many useful corrections, suggestions and comments. Asuka Yamashina gave me much love and encouragement along the way. Finally, this book is dedicated to my parents, Bernard and Terri Behrman, who brought me up with two qualities which mean a great deal to me, and were essential to the writing of this book: socialist politics and a love of music.

• The October revolution laid the foundations of a new culture taking everyone into consideration, and for that very reason immediately acquiring international significance. Even supposing for a moment that owing to unfavourable circumstances and hostile blows the Soviet regime should be temporarily overthrown, the inexpugnable impress of the October revolution would nevertheless remain upon the whole future development of mankind.[1]

FOR THE COLD WAR warriors, the history of the USSR was either one of unbroken tyranny or unbridled progress. But the USSR was, for many people, a strange paradox. It was the creation of a revolution led and supported by ordinary people, yet, within 20 years it had become one of the 20th century's bloodiest dictatorships. From the 1930s onwards, socialists struggled to reconcile these diametrically opposed aspects of the USSR. Leon Trotsky, one of the leaders of the revolution later exiled and then murdered on Stalin's orders, argued that the Stalinist dictatorship was the negation and not the continuation of the revolution.

Along with the political gains of the revolution, the new culture that Trotsky referred to was also destroyed by Stalinism. The explosion of new art that immediately followed the revolution has become known as the Golden Age, a period that brought forth Symbolism and Futurism among many other cultural movements. The names of Rodchenko, Kandinsky, Eisenstein, Meyerhold and Mayakovsky are just some of the great artists of the 20th century indelibly linked with this period. However, by degrees this revolutionary ferment in art was gradually choked off. Initially literature and the theatre were targeted; the final art form to come under attack was music. Music as the most abstract of art forms is the hardest to pin down for its actual meaning or political content, and thus came last in line for 'correction' by the Stalinist authorities. As one commentator on the Soviet music scene put it:

> Music is definitively prohibited literature when
> it starts to mumble; out of this – out of what has
> been definitively prohibited – a great and indepen-
> dent art is born.[2]

The attack on musical life, launched in Pravda in January 1936, centred on one particular individual, a composer who was not yet 30 but who had already achieved world fame as a leading modernist composer – Dmitri Dmitrievich Shostakovich.

No other Soviet artist was the whole history of the Soviet Union, from 1917 to the Stalinist counter-revolution, through World War II, the 'Thaw' of the 1950s right to the USSR's decay and eventual disintegration in the 1990s. So intertwined in his personal history, reputation and work, it has been argued that no composer since Ludwig van Beethoven has been 'so central to the history of his time, or has so consistently sought to express the sufferings and aspirations shared by millions of his contemporaries.' The themes of Shostakovich's music read like a 'syllabus for a course in modern political and social problems: war, revolutionary change, individual freedom, anti-Semitism, the role of women in society, dictatorship and disillusionment'.[3]

In addition, Shostakovich's music stands on many of the fault-lines which have divided artists throughout the 20th century, i.e. the tension between achieving a mass audience without giving in to commercialism or populism and the question of how to maintain tradition while being modern. Shostakovich is also the last of the 'Greats' in classical music: the last composer to have achieved a firm place in the repertoire of all major orchestras and ensembles across the world, a name known even to people with only a passing interest in classical music.

At the same time, Shostakovich appears to be something of an enigma, both as a person and in his music. Was he Communist or anti-Communist? Is his music highly sophisticated and nuanced, or populist and low-brow? Gerald McBurney, a composer who has worked on editing several Shostakovich scores, gave a lecture a few years ago entitled *Whose Shostakovich?*:

> Whose Shostakovich?' suggests a small and rather obvious pun. Not just 'Whose?' but 'Who's?' Not just 'To whom does Shostakovich belong?' but 'Who is he?[4]

One answer to the enigma is to dismiss any attempt to understand Shostakovich in anything other than a musical context: 'Shostakovich's music is his own and always sui generic. We should try to hear it as dispassionately as we do Palestrina's from counter-reformation Rome, or Wagner's from Bismarckian Germany'.[5]

Yet Palestrina would not be Palestrina without the Renaissance. Wagner himself was adamant that his own work was intended as a contribution to the unification of Germany and, I would argue, one cannot appreciate or fully understand Shostakovich's music without placing it in the context of the rise, decline and fall of the Russian revolution. There are other biographies which offer a far more rounded and detailed life of Shostakovich than this one. But what they all miss is a proper understanding of the dynamic of the Russian revolution and its eventual defeat. This in turn has led to some profound misunderstandings about the development of the style and content of his works. This book, therefore, aims to do two things: provide a short introduction to Shostakovich's life and works, but also offer a fresh and hopefully illuminating political framework with which to understand one of the most enigmatic artists of the 20th century.

IT HAS OFTEN BEEN the case that revolutions have led to cultural ferment. As a new society struggles to break through, the sense of liberation inspires artists to revolutionise their art and to reflect in myriad forms the spirit of revolution. In music the period surrounding the French revolution directly inspired the work of the 'holy trinity' of Joseph Haydn, Wolfgang Amadeus Mozart and Ludwig van Beethoven. In varying ways these composers expressed the dynamism of revolutionary change in their music. Sometimes this was made explicit, as in Mozart's *The Marriage of Figaro* (1784) and Beethoven's *Ninth Symphony* (1824). But more often the ideals of the era were expressed in more subtle and perhaps unconscious ways. What follows is a brief description of how classical music was shaped by revolution.[1]

From the middle of the 18th century the emerging bourgeoisie and progressive sections of the aristocracy replaced the church and the municipality as the primary patrons of music. This mainly took place with the growth of the public concert as the main venue for musical performance.[2]

The bourgeoisie liberated music from the confines of the aristocratic salon and the church, but instead by degrees

15

imposed the tyranny of the market. In addition, a mythology began to develop of the individual artistic genius isolated from the rest of society. This allowed for the emergence of the independent musician from Mozart and Beethoven onwards while making their social position all the more precarious. Mozart, for example, was the most popular musician of his day yet he died in poverty.

In Austria and Germany, the cradle of the classical tradition in music, there was no decisive break with the old order as occurred in France in 1789. Although they were invaded several times by Napoleon's armies, leading to the collapse of the Holy Roman Empire, the old feudal order quickly re-established itself, leaving the Austrian Empire, in particular, as a bastion of reaction for the rest of the 19th century. On the other hand, where some social progress was achieved, such as during Emperor Joseph II's rule in the 1780s or Otto von Bismarck's unification of Germany in 1871, it came from above in an often half-hearted manner. The tensions produced by a retarded development of society hobbled by a conservative bourgeois/aristocratic alliance decisively shaped classical form.

Classical form

There are two dominant aspects of classical form that distinguish it from the preceding baroque and subsequent modernist forms: a highly regulated 'tonality (a process that had begun in the baroque period but reached its most developed form in the classical era)', and a set of compositional forms, the most important of which is sonata form. If we look first at tonality, what we see is a system of fixed harmonic relationships that revolve around the 'well-tempered' scale of C, C sharp, B etc.[3] Each note has a series of undertones and overtones that in turn determine the various scales such as C major, F minor and so on. The counterposing of two conflicting keys or themes provides drama. However, this tension is ultimately resolved by concluding the piece in the same key as it began, and by thematic synthesis. It is this overall structure that gives that sense of resolution and finality that we associate with the grand symphonic tradition.

Sonata form has the simple progression, A-B-A. The first section is 'exposition' where the main themes are laid out. This is followed by a section where the themes are developed, placed in different keys, etc. Finally, we have the 'recapitulation' where the opening material is repeated, though this time with added elements from the 'development'. These two aspects of classical form, tonality and sonata, are the most basic, but there are a great many others that determine harmonic and thematic development, the composition of the ensemble, and so on. But to crudely summarise the essence of classical form, we can say that it is driven by a simple dialectical process: contrasting themes and keys are worked out in opposition to one another, but ultimately resolved achieving synthesis and thus resolution.

This musical form fitted perfectly the social conditions of a society experiencing the tensions and trauma associated with the transition from feudalism to capitalism, only in slow motion – the 'storm and stress' of conflict, but always reconciliation through harmonic and thematic resolution.

The classical/popular divide

By the end of the 19th century the bourgeoisie had firmly left its revolutionary past behind and had settled into its position as a ruling class. In its revolutionary phase the bourgeoisie sought to relate to and mobilise the masses.

Thus music, which occupied a particularly exalted position in revolutionary France, for example, was encouraged to be accessible and convey meaning to a mass audience. However, by the turn of the 20th century classical music had abandoned its earthy roots and become mystified, occupying an Olympian plane above the masses, in which the smug bourgeois could see himself reflected.

This change in attitude is epitomised by the growth of the Beethoven cult.[4] Where once he was celebrated for his revolutionary spirit, the cult removed him from his social context and deified him. This is the image that survives to this day, of a lonely individual, trapped in the prison of his deafness from where he alone revolutionised music. Stripped of its revolutionary content and context, the spirit of Beethoven came to be seen as divinely inspired, and thus of noble character. Shostakovich has suffered a more secular version of this myth in recent decades. It followed that the mark of a great work was its ability to rise above the mundane and the everyday. The nobler it was, the more it bore the mark of genius. Here we can see the beginning of the deep schism between 'high' and 'popular' art. Increasingly after Beethoven's death composers fell into two categories, popular tunesmiths such as Gioachino Rossini and Giuseppe Verdi who could appeal to the 'hoi polloi', and introverted purveyors of the romantic spirit, totally divorced from the material world, such as Robert Schumann and Johannes Brahms.

While classical music gradually became more elitist in those countries where capitalist states had become firmly established, eg France, Britain and Germany, the revolutionary spirit of classical music continued in those European nations still under the yoke of empire. Within the decaying Austro-Hungarian Empire, long-suppressed national cultures began to stir. Composers such as the Czechs Antonin Dvorak, Bedric Smetana and Leos Janacek and the Hungarians Bela Bartok and Zoltan Kodaly expressed an overtly nationalistic sentiment in their music. Within the Russian Empire as early as the mid-19th century Frederick Chopin had popularised the musical form of the 'polonaise', an expression of Polish nationalism. By the early 20th century Chopin had been succeeded by his compatriots Karol Szymanowski and Mieczyslaw Karlowicz. The Finnish national movement produced Jean Sibelius, whose *Finlandia* (1899) became an unofficial anthem of resistance to Russian domination.

While these national movements celebrated the weakening of the old empires, at the heart of the imperial countries themselves a sense of crisis at their declining power was becoming ever more evident in the music of the period. In Vienna visions of the grotesque and the banal were becoming ever more pronounced, first in the work of Gustav Mahler and then in the atonal music of Arnold Schoenberg and his followers. In Russia, Igor Stravinsky created works of shocking originality and violence in *The Firebird* (1910), *Petrushka* (1911) and especially *The Rite of Spring* (1913). Alexander Scriabin, meanwhile, was seeking transcendence through an increasingly spiritualist expression within his music.

Overall, the period from about 1880 until 1914 witnessed a growing sense of decay and anxiety in European classical music. The tensions this produced led to the growth of modernism as classical form began to break apart under the weight of the ever more extreme contradictions of society at large. The outbreak of World War I in 1914 was a horrible affirmation of the horrors presaged in the works of Mahler, Schoenberg and Stravinsky. The war was eventually brought to an end by a wave of revolution which was to define the rest of the 20th century and the life and work of one of its greatest composers, Dmitri Shostakovich.

Bliss was it in that dawn to be alive,
But to be young was very heaven!
– *William Wordsworth, 'The French revolution as
it appeared to enthusiasts at its commencement'*

SHOSTAKOVICH WAS born in St Petersburg in August 1906.
The Russia into which he was born was a very backward
country, to the extent that the priest at his christening had
the authority to veto the parent's choice of Jaroslav as
Shostakovich's first name, instead insisting on the 'good
Russian' name of Dmitri. But the Russia of the Tsars was
already beginning to experience its death throes. In the
year before Shostakovich's birth Russia became the site of
the first revolution of the 20th century, the 'dress rehearsal'
for 1917. On 9 [22] January 1905[1] the workers of St
Petersburg, led by Father Gapon, marched to the Tsar's
Winter Palace pleading for better conditions and moderate
political reforms. The response was brutal. Soldiers were
deployed and ordered to fire on the demonstration, killing
thousands. What became known as 'Bloody Sunday'
sparked off a series of political struggles that led in the
autumn of 1905 to the first appearance of the soviets.
These were elected bodies representing the workers in

their struggle with Tsarism. But they were more than that. They were the beginnings of a method of self-organisation by working people that could effectively challenge, and replace, the existing state.

In desperation, Tsar Nicholas II and his ministers promised democratic reforms and the creation of an elected parliament, the Duma, in return for the disarming of the workers and the disbandment of the soviets, which were in any case far more democratic than the proposed Duma. Many workers were prepared to accept this compromise, and it is not hard to see why. The autocratic Tsar had been forced to agree to demands from those considered the lowest in society. The sheer novelty of the situation and the exhilaration felt by the 'ordinary' people who had made this happen led many of them to believe that the Tsar's promises represented a victory already achieved.

Instead, once the revolution had been disarmed, Nicholas II promptly had its leaders arrested, jailed or sent into exile. Rather than a period of progress, the succeeding years witnessed severe reaction and repression. But beneath the surface revolutionary agitation continued, and bitterness towards Tsarist repression remained. In the arts the avant-garde movements of Futurism and Symbolism expressed both the continued desire to transcend the backwardness of Russian society, and the sense of deep unease present in an old society breaking at the seams. Shostakovich's upbringing took place within this society of tension and change.

Family background

Shostakovich's parents were educated members of the small middle class that had begun to develop in the cities. They were a musical family, with Shostakovich's mother a graduate of the prestigious St Petersburg Conservatoire. Beginning when he was nine years old, Shostakovich was taught by his mother to play the piano. Very quickly he demonstrated an unusual musical talent. He had perfect pitch (able to identify any note he heard), unusual sight-reading abilities, and a prodigious musical memory. Private instruction in music was arranged for the young Shostakovich, to prepare him to follow his mother into the St Petersburg Conservatoire. And by the age of just 16 he was already producing works of extraordinary quality such as *Theme & Variations* (1922) and *Three Fantastic Dances* (1922).

Shostakovich, like Mozart before him, was something of a child prodigy. However, there is nothing mystical about such gifts. Mozart too came from an intensely musical family. Of course, not every child who has the benefit of such an upbringing will end up with the talent of a Shostakovich or a Mozart. But equally, it is the case that nowadays music education is increasingly pushed to the margins. Governments prioritise 'job skills' over the personal development of the child, and the pace of life in industrialised capitalist societies leaves little time for most people to make music in the home or in the community. This means that such talent has become an even more exotic specimen than ever before.

But in addition to being a musical family the Shostakoviches were also socially aware, with a history of political radicalism. Shostakovich's paternal grandfather had joined one of Russia's earliest socialist organisations, *Zemlya i Volya* (Land and Freedom) in the 1860s, and was active enough to be arrested and exiled to Siberia for his suspected role in an attempted assassination of the Tsar. Shostakovich's Aunt Nadezhda was a member of the

Bolshevik Party for a period during the 1905 revolution. An uncle was a member of the Socialist revolutionary Party. Another uncle was an active Bolshevik who was often hidden in the Shostakovich family home in the years before the revolution. Shostakovich's parents were not themselves particularly radical or political. But they were typical of a liberal intelligentsia who yearned for Russia to achieve the democracy and cultural level of Western Europe.

1917

By early 1917 the Russian ruling class was again in crisis and facing renewed anger from below. Millions had died in the slaughter of World War I. There was famine in the countryside and conditions in the cities were also in sharp decline. To mark International Women's Day on 23 February [8 March] a strike and demonstration was organised by women textile workers in Petrograd (as St Petersburg had been renamed in 1914). The slogans raised were initially about bread, but resentment at the war and the deprivation it had produced bubbled up to the surface. The movement gathered pace and the strike movement spread. The soviets of 1905 were resurrected, again as organs of power representing the workers.

Once again the government decided to respond with violence. But this time when the Tsar ordered troops to restore order, many of them refused to fire on the protesters. Nicholas II's authority had been fatally weakened and he was forced to abdicate in favour of his brother. But by then the demands had moved beyond mere reform to revolutionary demands for a new republic, and the monarchy collapsed. Within the space of a week centuries of monarchical rule had been brought to an end, mourned by almost no one. A Provisional Government made up of capitalists, lawyers and parliamentarians was set up to replace the monarchy, with the aim of turning Russia into a liberal republic. Typical of the sentiment across Russia, Shostakovich's younger sister Zoya recalled their father returning home on the day the monarchy fell declaring 'Children, freedom!'

On 23 March [5 April] around one million people turned out in Petrograd for a funeral march in memory of those slaughtered by Tsarist troops during the February revolution. Prominent among the songs sung on that day was the revolutionary funeral march, *You Fell a Victim*. In among that huge crowd was the Shostakovich family. After they returned home that day, Shostakovich sat down at the piano and played *You Fell a Victim* for the rest of the family. In the following days the ten year old Shostakovich composed a piece for piano, *Funeral March in Memory of the Victims of the revolution*. At around the same time he also composed another solo piano piece entitled *Hymn to Liberty*.

According to Shostakovich himself, and the reminiscences of his sister Zoya, Shostakovich was present ten days later when Vladimir Lenin, on his return from exile, was greeted by crowds at the Finland Station. Many years later the Soviet authorities would claim that his *Funeral March* and presence at the Finland Station demonstrated Shostakovich's commitment to revolutionary ideals even in childhood. Equally, anti-Communists would later claim that actually the piece was intended in memory of victims of both the ancien regime and later of the Bolsheviks, and that the story of him being at the Finland Station was simply a myth. It seems highly unlikely that a boy of ten years old would have been weighing up the merits or otherwise of Lenin's speech at the Finland Station, even on the assumption that he was actually there. To suggest that his *Funeral March* was also a coded critique of the Bolsheviks when they were still a minority party, and seven months before they were in power, also suggests a preternatural political gift for which there is no evidence whatsoever. The most absurd of the claims concerning the story of Shostakovich at the Finland Station is that told by his sometime friend Lev Lebedinsky, who colluded in the dubious *Testimony*[2] following Shostakovich's death. Lebedinsky quoted Shostakovich as saying that he went to see Lenin's arrival at the Finland Station because 'I knew a dictator was arriving'.[3] These claims and counter-claims simply point up the fact that Shostakovich's life and works were so inextricably bound up with the revolution that even his ten year old thoughts and actions have become a point of controversy.

What is obvious and incontrovertible is that from the very beginning Shostakovich's life and music were shaped by the historic events of 1917. Indeed, it seems ridiculous to deny this fact as he was living in Petrograd, the very epicentre of the revolution. His schoolmates at the Shidlovskaya School included the sons of Alexander Kerensky, the head of the Provisional Government, as well as those of Trotsky and another leading Bolshevik, Lev Kamenev. What is remarkable is that he should have consciously sought to express the events happening around him in his music, even at such a young age. By contrast, Sergei Prokofiev, fifteen years older than Shostakovich and already an accomplished musician, welcomed the outbreak of revolution in February yet spent the summer of that epochal year composing a symphony in the style of Haydn.

The concern to reflect the 'world outside' in music was to be a current running through Shostakovich's works almost until the end of his life. This aspect of his music, and the fact that it occurred so early in his development, is particularly striking in the context of classical music up to this time. As discussed in the previous chapter, for almost a century classical music had been moving ever further from social concerns. The leading composers by this time, Claude Debussy, Stravinsky, Schoenberg, all saw music as something above or outside of everyday life. The reconnection between music and wider social and political life was to be part of Shostakovich's greatness as a composer. But credit for this must also go to the revolution and those who made it. Just as socialism is about destroying the social and economic divisions within society, so too it aims to break down the barriers that have grown up in class society between art and everyday life. In Russia in the early revolutionary period concerts organised by trade unions were given by the great opera singer Feodor Chaliapin and the Bolshoi Ballet for crowds of workers eager to absorb the culture that had hitherto been denied them by bourgeois society. On walls of the major cities, expressionist paintings appeared, while in the streets improvised sculptures celebrating the revolution were erected by countless anonymous 'ordinary' people.[4] And in order to overcome the dire shortage of paper, poets, including Vladimir Mayakovsky, recited their works on street corners.

The soviets, not the Provisional Government, had made the revolution. Yet the soviets, which now included representatives of the soldiers and the peasants as well as the working class, at first did not know what to do with the power they had won and handed executive power to the Provisional Government. This was due to a combination of a lack of political leadership and a lifetime of being told that working people like themselves were unable or unfit to be in charge. But crucially and perhaps remembering the betrayal of the soviets in 1905, the soviets of 1917 refused to disband. The tension between these two rival centres of authority led to eight months of dual power.

Dual power by its nature could not survive for long. Either the Provisional Government or the soviets had to win the sole right to govern. Initially the Provisional Government seemed to be stabilising. The key test for the new government was the question of the war. But instead of ending

Lenin speaks to the crowd while Trotsky waits. Russia, 1918

the slaughter, it ordered new offensives. Soldiers left the battlefield in droves and returned home to their cities and villages. By the summer the Provisional Government was fast losing its authority. In desperation it rounded up and arrested the most revolutionary elements, including the leadership of the increasingly popular Bolshevik Party. In

August military officers led by General Kornilov attempted a coup, with the aim of destroying both the soviets and the Provisional Government and burying the revolution. The Provisional Government was now forced to rely on the soviets and the growing authority of the Bolsheviks to head off the coup.

The Kornilov coup was easily defeated. But, it was from this point on that the revolution entered its decisive phase. The Bolsheviks had proved in practice that they were loyal to the revolution and to the soviets. Having already shown itself to be morally bankrupt in continuing the war, the Provisional Government now stood exposed as politically bankrupt, unable to effectively defend even a liberal republic. By September the Bolsheviks had won a majority in the soviets. They were now in a position to organise for a Soviet seizure of power.

On the night of 25 October [7 November] the Military revolutionary Committee, elected by the soviets, rose in insurrection. Within hours the government had fallen. The insurrection was timed to coincide with the Congress of the soviets, and the following day the Military revolutionary Committee handed power to the soviets which in turn voted to ratify the insurrection. The Russian Soviet Republic was declared. The first actions of the new government included immediate withdrawal from the war, ratification of the peasant seizures of land from the big landowners and the eight-hour day.

The insurrection of October 1917 was clearly not, as is often asserted, a military coup by Lenin and the Bolsheviks. Certainly the party of Lenin was the principle inspirer and organiser of the soviet seizure of power; but it was through the soviets, made up of the representatives of the workers, peasants and soldiers, that the new republic was established and organised. Victor Serge has described how, in the period following the insurrection, when the Soviet state was still at an embryonic stage, rank and file workers took the initiative in setting up new forms of organisation to replace those of the Provisional Government. In turn, once the new government had begun to stabilise, a huge programme of education and social liberalisation was set in train. Decades before all the Western liberal democracies, schools for children with learning difficulties and adult educational courses were set up. Women won full equal rights with men, and the right to abortion and divorce on demand. Without an understanding of the reality of liberation and social progress that characterised the Soviet Republic in its early years, it is impossible to comprehend the enormous artistic flowering of the decade that followed. The 'Golden Age' of Russian art and culture became the inspiration for the young Shostakovich to create his first masterpieces. And within a decade Shostakovich would become one of the principal drivers behind this Golden Age.

3: The Golden Age

In 1919 SHOSTAKOVICH gained entry to the Petrograd Conservatoire. There he studied piano and composition. Among his teachers was the famous composer and musical heir to Nicolai Rimsky-Korsakov, Alexander Glazunov, who took a special interest in Shostakovich's development. Shostakovich's talent as a pianist was of such a high standard that as his graduation from the Conservatoire approached ten years later he was still considering whether to pursue a career as a concert pianist rather than as a composer. As it happened, he maintained a dual career as both performer and composer until the late 1950s when illness prevented him from continuing to play the piano. Luckily, there are a number of recordings of him playing his own compositions. His childhood friend Leo Arnshtam recalled something of the young Shostakovich's playing while at the Conservatoire, capturing an aspect of his musical style which remained throughout his life:

> One was struck by his...particularly enhanced rhythmic sense... This rhythmic sense lay at the very core of Shostakovich's world, and it was forged by the rhythm and pace of the revolution'.[1]

In the ten to fifteen years immediately following the revolution, Russia went from being the most culturally backward country in Europe to becoming a hub of cultural experimentalism and mass popular engagement with the arts. Communism is usually presented as aspiring to a cultural monolithism, with the sole banal aim of glorifying the revolution itself. But in this early period, and encouraged by the Soviet authorities, there was a flowering of many different styles and approaches to art including Futurism, Constructivism and Symbolism. Russia became the home of some of the first uses of new techniques such as montage in film and electronica in music. There were debates over the uses and purpose of art within wider society. In particular, arguments raged over whether bourgeois art should be celebrated and built upon, or whether a 'proletarian state' should be solely concerned with promoting 'proletarian art'. In short, revolutionary Russia produced an exciting and varied ferment in cultural life.

On the musical scene, the 1920s saw the birth of Persimfans,[2] an experiment with a modern orchestra without a conductor where the interpretation of pieces was instead collectively discussed by the musicians. Leon Theremin invented an instrument using radio waves which was the world's first electronic musical instrument. In fact, Theremin at one point taught Lenin how to play it and Shostakovich was to employ the theremin in his score for the movie *Alone* (1930). Among some of the more weird and wonderful compositions that emerged from the USSR of the 1920s were pieces such as *The Iron Foundry* (1927) by Alexander Mosolov, and Arseny Avraamov's *Symphony of Sirens* (1922) which employed a whole range of unorthodox sounds and instruments. Mikhail Druskin, a fellow student of Shostakovich during this decade, described the period as 'an explosion of creative energy'.[3] The debates about the role of art in the revolution coalesced in the musical scene around two rival organisations both formed in 1923, the Russian Association of Proletarian Musicians (RAPM) and the Association for Contemporary Music (ASM). RAPM was part of the 'proletkult' movement. Proletkult was dedicated to the idea that alongside the smashing of the bourgeois state the workers' state should also dispense with bourgeois art. Proletkult was summed up by the proletkultist poet Mayakovsky:

> Spit on rhymes and arias and the rose bush and other such mawkishness from the arsenal of the arts... Give us new forms![4]

While Lenin was equivocal about proletkult, Trotsky was firmly opposed to it for two reasons. The first was that the 'proletarian state' was aimed at the abolition of all classes including the working class itself, in the interests of a classless society. Therefore a proletarian culture, by the time it had been constructed, would be obsolete. Second, Trotsky argued that, as with philosophy and industrial techniques, so too the very best of what bourgeois society had produced should be appropriated for all, and developed to its furthest extent.

The ASM followed Trotsky's outlook by championing the Western European avant-garde music of composers such as Mahler, Schoenberg, Alban Berg and Paul Hindemith. The ASM also sought to promote the most advanced and newest forms of music, both Russian and foreign. Shostakovich was a supporter of the ASM which was based in Moscow, and when a branch (LASM) was set up in his home city of Leningrad (as Petrograd had been renamed in 1924) in 1926 he was one of its founding members. The strong links between the LASM and Shostakovich are attested to by the fact that the very first symphonic concert of the LASM was the premiere of his *First Symphony* (1925). And in December 1926 Shostakovich performed the premiere of his *First Piano Sonata* (1926) at an LASM concert.

What is important to stress is that for Shostakovich, and certainly for the leading figures of the ASM such as Boris Asafiev, the celebration of experimentalism and the avant-garde did not preclude, for want of a better term, 'accessibility' to a mass audience. Beginning somewhere around the middle of the 19th century, but certainly by the 1920s, 'classical' music was fast becoming ghettoised. In the late 1920s when Alban Berg invited George Gershwin to play some of his music for assembled guests in Vienna, Gershwin, embarrassed before one of the leading lights of the European avant-garde, excused himself on the grounds that his works were nothing but popular tunes. Berg's admirable response that 'music is music' would have been meaningless to a Bach or a Beethoven. Undoubtedly there had always been different types of music, church music, dance music, love songs etc, seen as appropriate for different occasions and settings, but the idea that certain forms of music were music and others mere entertainment would have been unthinkable in earlier societies.

This artificial division is symptomatic of capitalist society's rigid division of labour as reflected in the arts: one is either a manual worker or an intellectual. Equally a musician can either be an entertainer or an artist but not both. In addition, the way in which capitalism turns everything produced in society into a commodity to be marketed and sold inevitably leads to an artificial 'nichefication' of culture. By creating a series of well-defined markets, competing firms which are producing essentially the same product can carve out distinct parts of society with which to target their products, and maintain their market share. Likewise cultural 'scenes' may initially grow up as mutually influencing trends, but increasingly they become self-contained ghettos defined by a spurious sense of identity that is in turn created by the capitalist peddlers of the cultural products which connect artists to audience. The music historian Henry Raynor argued that with the development of capitalism:

> [Western music] became increasingly the pleasure of a cultured elite rather than an immediate communication between men and women. It was not long before the ambitious composer discovered that the provision of dance music and easy-going entertainment was beneath his dignity, and a divided society was left to make do with a divided art.[5]

Shostakovich always refused to accept these divisions. He proudly declared his love of music 'from Bach to Offenbach', and his compositions included hit tunes, jazz and film scores as well as symphonies and quartets. Indeed, one of the biggest hit tunes of the 1930s in the USSR was his *Song of the Counterplan* (1932). This began as part of a score for a Stalinist propaganda film about workers producing more than the state target during the First Five Year Plan. The tune was so catchy it travelled the Atlantic and in 1942 was turned into the United Nations song by Harold Rome. A year later the music was used in the Judy Garland and Gene Kelly musical *Thousands Cheer* and became a hit in the USA too. From agitprop pop to MGM in a decade! As a result of his democratic attitude to music, until the 1990s Shostakovich had a marginal status in academic circles. In addition, musicologists refused to accept the explicit historical and political themes of his work, believing that his work belonged to the 'concertgoer rather than the serious scholar'.[6]

The revolutionary movement that sought to abolish the division of society into classes and forms of labour inspired the pursuit of a culture that left behind the increasing ghettoisation of different types of art. And this liberation of culture from 'nichefication' was a crucial dynamic of revolutionary art missing from the 'proletkult' view. In this sense, Shostakovich's irrepressible eclecticism and refusal to be pigeonholed as either a 'serious' or a 'popular' composer marks him as a true child of the revolution.

Film Music

Shostakovich's pianistic skills were to come to the aid of his family when in 1922 his father died unexpectedly. The family found themselves in dire financial straits, and Shostakovich was forced to combine his studies with work as a pianist accompanying silent films at the cinema. This work was to last several years, and Shostakovich seems, for the most part, to have hated the experience. The work was hard (playing continuously for hours on end) and not particularly rewarding, either artistically or financially. However, it began a lifelong creative association between Shostakovich and the cinema. Not only was he to produce dozens of scores for films over the next half century, but this formative experience undoubtedly left its mark on the 'Shostakovich style'. Some of his outstanding film scores are those for *The New Babylon* (1929), *The Gadfly* (1955) and *King Lear* (1970). Throughout his work, whether it is symphonies, concertos or chamber music, there is often a pronounced cinematic element to it. He frequently dropped in vivid musical descriptions of dramatic actions such as a moving crowd, bombing raids, drunken partying, etc. In addition, certain pieces appear to be structured in the manner of a series of acoustic tableaux moving before our ears. This is particularly evident in his *Second, Seventh* and *Eleventh* symphonies, the *Eighth String Quartet* and the two *Cello Concertos*. For musical snobs this stylistic trait has been a stick with which to beat Shostakovich. Supposedly, this shows his inability to write 'absolute' music that did not have to rely on extra-musical devices or imagery.

This hostility to film music or any music which relies on extra-musical imagery displays not just snobbishness but a lack of understanding of music history. In every musical culture, be it Ancient Greek theatre, Indian ragas, African ritual dances or the European classical tradition, music has in most cases been related to some extra-musical element. This might be as accompaniment to a play, a rite of passage or spiritual enlightenment. 'Music for music's sake' is a myth, and moreover meaningless. Every composition of Johann Sebastian Bach's was dedicated to the Lutheran God, Beethoven's 'heroic style' was only made possible in the context of the French revolution and Richard Wagner's 'artwork of the future' was consciously developed as part of the German nationalist movement of the middle of the 19th century. And these are just a few examples. Of course, music that exploits the form simply to evoke extra-musical ideas without concern for the unique qualities of music itself will end up as banal. The point is that music must form a reciprocal relationship between itself and the world, whether it be themes of politics, love, nature, spirituality or whatever. Music which fails to relate beyond itself becomes either trivial, as is often the case in the work of Erik Satie, or obtuse, as is evident in much of the work of the post Second World War European avant-garde.

But snobbery towards music for the cinema also often

betrays hostility towards an art form of a mass or popular character. No one seems to have a problem with Mozart using music to create the sound effect of a thunderstorm in *Don Giovanni* (1787), or Beethoven describing a funeral procession in his *Third Symphony*. Presumably they gain a pass simply for being Mozart and Beethoven, and because they belong to a genre designated as 'high art'. But cinema in the 20th century (arguably playing a similar role within mass culture to opera in the 19th century)[7] has produced musical scores of subtlety and sophistication that can hold their own against a Verdi or Giacomo Puccini. Think for example of Bernard Hermann's score for Alfred Hitchcock's *Vertigo* (1958), Prokofiev's music for Eisenstein's *Alexander Nevsky* (1938) or Wendy Carlos's work on Stanley Kubrick's *A Clockwork Orange* (1971). It seems to me that Shostakovich's ability to move easily from writing cinema scores, using techniques of symphonic form, to writing symphonic works employing the dramatic imagery of the moving image is a mark of great talent, rather than a lack of it. Most importantly, it places Shostakovich as someone able to traverse the 'high art/popular culture' schism mentioned earlier. Perhaps the most tantalising result of Shostakovich's musical engagement with the cinema is the 1933 animated film *The Tale of the Priest and his Servant Balda*. The animator Mikhail Tsekhanovsky lost his contract with Lenfilm before completion. The surviving fragment suggests a marvellously riotous and surreal experiment in animation. It is highly likely that Tsekhanovsky's contract was ended due to the cultural counter-revolution of Socialist Realism which was then getting into gear. Luckily Shostakovich's music for the film survives as a concert suite, and it vividly demonstrates contemporary descriptions of the 'hooliganism' in his early works.

It was Shostakovich's graduation piece which first made his name famous and set him on the path to a career as a composer. The terrific success of the premiere of his *First Symphony* (1925) confirmed Shostakovich, still only 19 years old, as a composer with the talent to achieve greatness. Conductors of the stature of, and as varied in taste as Bruno Walter, Leopold Stokowski, Otto Klemperer and Arturo Toscanini immediately took the piece into their repertoire. The breadth of appreciation of the *First Symphony* is also shown in its promotion by Darius Milhaud and Alban Berg, composers representing diametrically opposed wings of early-20th century modernism. But to appreciate the full extent of Shostakovich's achievement in this work it is necessary to give a brief account of the state of symphonic form at this time.

From the early 19th century onwards the symphony had become the pre-eminent form for expressing grand themes in music. Beethoven celebrated the heroic grandeur and struggle of the French revolution in his *Third Symphony* (1803), and with his hymn to Enlightenment ideals in the *Ninth Symphony* (1824) set a bar against which every composer of symphonies had to measure themselves.

By the end of the century Mahler, by juxtaposing banal musical themes with a highly developed romanticism and stretching harmonic tension almost to breaking point, had transformed the symphony into a highly complex form that expressed the angst and confusion of an age that promised so much in terms of scientific and industrial progress, yet created a world ever more alienated and perverse.

Many composers felt that with Mahler the symphony had reached its end point. Looked at in purely musical terms they felt that the central dynamic of the symphony – the use of tension between contrasting themes and keys – had been exploited to its fullest extent. In this way the symphonic form had been extended to its breaking point, and belonged to history along with the motet and the baroque suite. During the 1920s the composers still writing symphonies in the grand tradition were those of a harmonically conservative bent such as Jean Sibelius, Ralph Vaughan Williams, and Carl Nielsen. The only modernist attempts at symphonies, such as Stravinsky's *Symphonies of Wind Instruments* (1920) and Anton Webern's *Symphony* (1928), consciously sought to deflate the form of any grand, rhetorical or social content.

There were also extra-musical reasons for the growing sense that the symphony was outmoded. One of the major aspects of the symphony was its sense of universalism and resolution. It is no accident that the symphony should have achieved its classical form during the age of Enlightenment and bourgeois revolution. The ideals of the Enlightenment promoted the concept of a universal brotherhood of man, thus breaking from the notion of humanity rigidly divided by birth and status. By the beginning of the 20th century the promise of 'brotherhood, equality and freedom' had become mere hollow rhetoric.

With the carnage and brutality of World War I it had become clear that the industrial and scientific progress of capitalism had led not to an era of universalist humanism, but to horror on a previously unimaginable scale. Rather than bringing humanity closer together, the modern world was driving people apart, not just at the level of nations fighting all-out wars, but also at the level of everyday life. Industrial cities produced, on the one hand, the greatest conglomerations of human beings, yet on the other hand, had created conditions of squalor and alienation hitherto unknown. The extremities of these social contradictions could no longer be adequately expressed in the closed and resolvable forms of the symphony. This argument was put in its most sophisticated form by the Marxist philosopher Theodore Adorno.[1]

This pessimism and ennui was for a period transcended by the hopes of the Russian revolution. The ripples of the events in Russia in 1917 extended as far as Western Europe and China over the following decade with revolutionary challenges to power, in many cases coming tantalisingly close to victory. As late as 1937 in Spain the prospect of socialist revolution in Europe seemed to be on the agenda. Many composers reacted to this revolutionary hope through an explicit commitment to radical politics, as was the case with Kurt Weill and Hanns Eisler. Many others remained apolitical but nevertheless expressed the turbulence, the shattering of illusions and the possibilities of an alternative existence in their music; the work of Hindemith and Stravinsky comes to mind in this respect. There were, of course others, usually of an older generation, who were unable to cope with the radical uncertainties of a new era, and clung in their music to an old fashioned harmonic language and set of musical forms. This was particularly the case with Edward Elgar and Shostakovich's teacher Alexander Glazunov, although it must be said that Glazunov was able to see beyond his own prejudices. His reaction to Shostakovich's *First Symphony* was, 'Of course the work shows great talent, but I don't understand it'.[2]

At various times Shostakovich was accused of possessing the vices of being too political in his music, or of being not political enough; too avant-garde or too traditional; esoteric or populist. What is undoubtedly the case is that he was able to communicate clearly to his audience about the turbulent social and political times in which he lived without being hectoring or obvious. He was able to use new forms of musical expression without losing the thread of the musical tradition he inherited. Further, he was able to do that hardest of things, to create a completely unique and recognisable musical style. And, perhaps most importantly in terms of the difficulties experienced by artists in the 20th century, Shostakovich managed to communicate effectively with a mass audience without becoming banal or populist. This is not to say that he always managed to avoid these traps, but he was able to achieve these things consistently and bravely in spite of levels of artistic, social and political pressure that broke or irretrievably compromised many of his contemporaries.

What is amazing about his *First Symphony* is that he was able to demonstrate these qualities so early in his career and at such a young age. The first movement begins searchingly but quickly gathers pace and bursts into life with spiky dance-like rhythms. The second movement has the character of a light-hearted dance, but with a few abrupt piano chords (an unusual choice of instrument for a symphony) just before the end, the whole mood shifts to a darker tone. This mood continues into the slow movement, while the final movement veers between this tension and darkness and the hope and playfulness of the earlier movements. The symphony as a whole displays a firm grasp of structure, and a brilliant use of orchestration. These are elements so crucial to the traditional symphonic form, yet so hard to achieve. Stylistically, it holds the attention with a wonderful sense of rhythm and drama. Harmonically, it is angular and searching which again grabs the listener's attention. All these aspects of style and harmony, of drama and abruptly shifting moods, were to carry through to his last symphony over 40 years later. Shostakovich had, at the age of just 19, found his own unique musical voice, something that usually takes musicians years to achieve. Such revolutionary composers as Beethoven, Wagner and Schoenberg were in their 30s by the time they had fully developed their own distinct musical voice. It would also not be an exaggeration to say that Shostakovich was the key link in maintaining the grand symphony as a living form in the 20th century. But the brightness and eventual optimism of the *First Symphony* suggest something else too. Mstislav Rostropovich, the cellist, conductor and close friend of Shostakovich, as well as also being very anti-communist, was able to see the significance of the piece:

> [*The First Symphony*] is a brilliant call to freedom and the future... At the time that he wrote it, he was full of hope for his own artistic future. And then there was the more general hope inspired by the revolution, namely, that it would bring freedom and new opportunities.[3]

Second Symphony

The early optimism and hope inspired by the revolution carried over into the *Second Symphony: To October* (1927), and his *Third Symphony: The First of May* (1929). As is clear from their subtitles, these works were explicit celebrations of the revolution itself. The *Second Symphony* was commissioned by the Soviet government as part of the 10th anniversary celebrations of the revolution, and went on to win a prize from the Leningrad Philharmonic for the best composition of those celebrations. It is another highly adventurous work, with an eerie opening that stylistically could easily have been composed any time over the subsequent half-century and yet still have been considered cutting-edge. It is a deliberately challenging work with strange harmonies, obscure melodies and an unorthodox development. But it was enormously popular when it was first performed, and in my opinion it is one of the very best combinations of politics and music from the 20th century. The inspiration of the Russian revolution and of revolutionary socialism generally inspired many composers to express commitment to those ideals in music. But none, in my opinion, succeeded in uniting form and content as well as this symphony. While there are many works which express the horrors of capitalism, or resistance to oppression, there has been a dearth of works which evoke the hope of revolution, and even among these few works hardly any are successful as both music and political expression. Composers were either so intent on getting the political message across that they composed pieces that were banal and bombastic, such is the case with Erwin Schulhoff's oratorio *The Communist Manifesto* (1933). At the other extreme the musical language was so abstruse that it obscured the revolutionary content of the work, as with Luigi Nono's *Al Gran Sole Carico d'Amore* (1974).

The reason for this paucity of works that evoked the sprit of socialist revolution, and did so successfully, is easy to account for. Apart from Russia in 1917, while there have been many attempts and near-misses, there has not been a successful socialist revolution anywhere else. And even in Russia, the revolution lasted at most ten years before Stalinism began to strangle it. So very few composers have had the direct experience of revolution, even fewer the talent to express it as vividly as Shostakovich does in his *Second Symphony*.

But there is also a specifically musical aspect to the problem of evoking socialist revolution in classical music. How exactly does one express in music what, in Karl Marx's phrase, was a situation where 'the free development of each was the precondition for the free development of all'? By contrast the bourgeois revolutions celebrated the individual in splendid isolation. Think of the idolisation of Napoleon and Beethoven. Alternatively the collective was celebrated in the abstract notion of universal brotherhood. Individual heroism and a single collective can easily be expressed in classical form; such are the origins of the concerto for solo instrument, and the grand symphony. But how to express in music a mass of recognisable individuals who come together as a collective force? In Beethoven's great paean to revolution, his *Ninth Symphony*, it is a single musical narrative that is followed throughout. Shostakovich's closest friend, the musicologist Ivan Sollertinsky, put the case for how the symphony could be appropriated for this new society:

> Symphonism as a method (not as the canonisation
> of a genre) in its basis is collectivist; it draws
> its material not from 'tradition' but from living
> everyday music, from songs of the street, rejecting

on principle refinement, or a recherché quality of
musical material...

And now the question poses itself: is symphonism
any use to us? The answer, I think, is pre-
determined; of course, it is precisely our epoch,
with its huge gamut of feelings, with its quantity
of collectivizing ideas, that is able to continue the
development of the symphonic idea as a method
of collectivising experiences. Music is capable of
solving this problem like nothing else.[4]

Crucial to Sollertinsky's formulation is the incorporation
of 'everyday' music, which was a key component of
Shostakovich's symphonies.

In his *Second Symphony* Shostakovich comes closer than
anyone before or since to evoking the essence of socialist
revolution in classical form. The symphony has a highly
unorthodox form, using just one movement as opposed
to the standard four. The only other symphony up to this
point which used just one movement was Sibelius' very
different *Seventh Symphony* (1924). Shostakovich takes
us in one continuous sweep from a murky opening with
gradually building tension, conjuring up the image of day
breaking on a city filled with tension. Without a break we
are suddenly amid a multiplicity of voices in the orchestra
moving towards a frenzy, which is then overlaid with a
'rat-a-tat-tat' in the percussion unmistakably evoking
the army firing on the assembled masses. The music then
retreats as if in despair before rising phoenix-like with
the chorus celebrating the victory of 'October'. In just
20 minutes the listener is transported to the city square,
the demonstrations, the pitched battles and the feeling of
victorious liberation of a socialist revolution. As if this
were not enough, Shostakovich fearlessly employs radical

modernist harmonies, thus making this a symphony firmly of the 20th and not the 19th century. In short, the *Second Symphony* is a work of true genius and a unique achievement in combining a vivid description of socialist revolution with the grand symphonic form. The one drawback of the piece is the text of the finale, a poem by Aleksander Bezymensky. Apparently Shostakovich did not like it. With lines such as, 'O Lenin! You forged the will of the suffering', it is not hard to see why.

Yet the *Second Symphony*, following its initial success, all but vanished from the repertoire both in the USSR and abroad. Even many years later Yakov Milkis, violinist in the Leningrad Philharmonic from 1957 to 1974 reported that the *Second Symphony* and *Third Symphony* were the only ones of Shostakovich's not to be performed. Even today these are the least performed of Shostakovich's 15 symphonies. Outside of the USSR the *Second Symphony's* explicit celebration of workers' revolution was hardly likely to find a place in concert halls frequented by the middle and upper classes. Although curiously Leopold Stokowski, who was committed to bringing classical music to a mass audience, most famously in his contribution to Disney's Fantasia, and who was given to playing the Internationale at concerts of his Philadelphia Orchestra (gaining as a result a large FBI file), was one of the few conductors to champion the work. In the USSR the symphony's experimentalism was soon to fall out of favour as the revolution began to be hollowed out and turned into a grotesque parody of itself. The RAPM denounced the Second Symphony as 'decadent' and 'formalist', epithets that would soon become used with nauseating regularity as the Stalinist counter-revolution became entrenched within Soviet life.

Not for the last time the fate of Shostakovich and his music became intimately entwined with the changing fortunes of the revolution. But also, as would repeatedly be the case over the years, he bravely asserted his view of art. Writing publicly shortly after the first performances of the *Second Symphony* he described his artistic goals:

> The reception given to 'October' by the working public convinced me that the projected path is the right one. I compose always being guided by the following considerations. Accessibility and intelligibility to the mass listener, for only the mass listener is the sole real appreciator of music, for music is one of the most mass-scale arts. In this I consider it my duty to fight against the turgid flow of musical pornography poured upon the head of the mass listener under the pretext of 'intelligibility' and 'comprehensibility'.[6]

At the centre of the Avant-Garde

Shostakovich eventually finished his studies at the Leningrad Conservatoire in 1928. But already he was acknowledged as one of the brightest stars of his generation, with a growing international reputation. And he was at the very centre of the cultural avant-garde. Impressed by his *First Symphony*, in 1928 Vsevolod Meyerhold, the leading innovator in Russian theatre, invited Shostakovich to become music director of his theatre. Meyerhold was often considered as the Russian Brecht, an ideologically committed dramatist who wanted to break down the invisible wall between performers and audience. Several years before the revolution, Meyerhold was agitating for a new theatrical style which would break through the staid naturalism which was then prevalent

Rehearsing 'The Bed Bug', 1929, seated Shostakovich and Meyerhold, standing Mayakovsky and Rodchenko.

in the theatre. As such he was a pioneer of symbolism. Meyerhold enthusiastically welcomed the revolution, and identified his radical artistic ideals with it. Shostakovich and Meyerhold forged a close friendship that lasted until Meyerhold's arrest and execution during the purges a decade later.

In 1929 Shostakovich was engaged to write the music for Meyerhold's production of *The Bedbug* written by Vladimir Mayakovsky, one of the leading Soviet poets of the 1920s. Myakovsky, like Meyerhold, also gained inspiration from the revolution in developing a new and liberated art. The stage design for *The Bedbug* was by Alexander Rodchenko, whose artwork using abstract lines and shapes has since become the ubiquitous symbol of the early Soviet artistic avant-garde.

The fact that Shostakovich, still only 22, was chosen to collaborate with these leading lights of the Soviet avant-garde is a testimony to his extraordinary talent. But it also confirms his commitment to a radically experimental edge in his art. This is evident in the music with its angular constructivist rhythms and harmonies. Two other aspects of style which dominate the score for *The Bedbug* would become central to the Shostakovich style for the rest of his life. Jazz idiom, then new and often challenging, runs through the piece, as does a sarcastic and mocking style. Perhaps the zenith of Shostakovich's melding of jazz with classical music is his exhilarating *Concerto for Piano, Trumpet and Strings* (1933). Shostakovich was always a great lover of jazz, but the fact that he was quite happy to write music that was 'popular' and 'dirty' while also producing 'high art' in his symphonic and operatic works once again shows a complete lack of elitism in his approach to music. In this, Shostakovich was at one with his collaborators in the Soviet avant-garde. Mayakovsky's programme note for *The Bedbug* included the following manifesto:

Theatres
Are not
Stony piles
For unravelling
Of miniature souls.
Let's strip such individuation
Of its robes.
Make art
From all
For all!

They, like Shostakovich, did not look down on their audience, nor did they pander to their audience by producing 'easy' or 'comfortable' art. In contrast to this ideal of 'art for all', Schoenberg was typical of the Western European avant-gardists when he said, 'If it is art, it is not for all, and if it is for all, it is not art'.[7]

Shostakovich threw himself into this milieu of artists committed to the development of a new art that was part of, and essentially driven by the ideals of socialist liberation. In 1929 he joined TRAM, a militant political theatre collective following Brechtian ideas, writing music for many of their productions. Henry Orlov captures the essence of the group of Soviet artists, within which he includes Shostakovich together with Meyerhold, Myakovsky and the filmmaker Sergei Eisenstein,

> All were stimulated to revolutionise their art but also to reach beyond art, as their ultimate goal was the renewal of life: breaking the shackles of submission and slavish thinking...Their art was not an end in itself but a means to the future they envisioned.[9]

Whatever may have been the case later on his life, during the late 1920s and early 1930s Shostakovich was clearly a believer in the Communist ideal. Most importantly he reflected the very best of the sprit of those ideals in his music.

Shostakovich: Socialism, Stalin & Symphonies

THE FAILURE OF THE Russian revolution to spread internationally had by the end of the 1920s left the USSR isolated. As predicted by Lenin and other leading Bolsheviks the failure to spread was to lead to the revolution's defeat, but in a way that they had not expected. Defeat did not come at the hands of invading armies or a counter-revolution from the old ruling class; both of these threats had been successfully faced down in the early 1920s. Instead, weakened by civil war and economic backwardness, the revolution began to degenerate from within. The working class who had made the revolution, in whose name the Soviet state was set up, had been effectively decimated by the civil war of 1918-21, and the famine caused by it.

In the Communist Party an increasing authoritarianism began to take hold. At first this was fiercely resisted from within the party itself. Lenin's final political act was to launch an attack on the increasing bureaucratisation of the party and the Soviet state. Specifically, he demanded the removal of Stalin as general secretary of the Party. It was already becoming clear that the revolution was being corrupted from within. Tragically Lenin died in 1924 before he could pursue this fight to preserve the gains of the revolution. Whether he would have succeeded had he lived is debatable. The fate of the revolution depended not on the machinations and arguments between individuals at the top, but instead depended crucially on the eventual failure or success of the revolution abroad. With the defeat of the workers' uprising in Germany in November 1923, those militants who had survived the privations of the civil war became further demoralised. Lenin and Trotsky's position rested on the need for the working class to remain active in its own self-interests. But the working class of Russia was spiritually broken by the mid-1920s. Stalin, on the other hand, who argued for a stronger state administration and control, reflected a defeatist acceptance of a retreat from self-rule to governance from above.

But the memory of 1917 remained alive, and the Stalin counter-revolution was continually resisted within the Communist Party. At first, this took the form of factional struggles with the bureaucratic element around Stalin triumphant. First the Left Opposition led by Trotsky was defeated, and Trotsky was removed from his position as head of the Red Army, then from the ruling Politburo and then from the Central Committee. The defeat of the Chinese revolution in late 1927 was the basis for Stalin's victory over the Bolshevik tradition. In short order, Trotsky and his followers were expelled from the party, and Trotsky was sent into exile. Stalin then turned on and defeated the Right Opposition led by Nicolai Bukharin.

Stalin's doctrine of 'socialism in one country' signalled the end of the Russian Communist Party's commitment to revolution. The Five Year Plan announced by Stalin in 1928 marked a shift from an economic policy dedicated to increasing consumption for the population, to a policy that prioritised production and competition with the West.[1] The result was mass starvation and the beginnings of a system of slave labour. The ruling party's name remained the same, but its guiding principle of working class self-emancipation, and its spirit of vigorous internal debate were dead. The only thing left of the Bolsheviks of 1917 was some of the personnel. Starting from the grass-roots upwards, these people would in increasing numbers and with increasing ferocity also end up dead at the hands of a new ruling class headed by Stalin, the most mediocre figure within the Bolshevik leadership. In the words of Victor Serge, a 'river of blood' separated the party of Lenin from that of Stalin.

At first the battle for the soul of the revolution centred on questions of economic policy and the political strategy of the Communist International. Cultural questions were thus, for a time, left relatively untouched by the Stalin counter-revolution. As a result the cultural gains of 1917, namely the flourishing of experimentalism and vigorous and free debate between different schools of thought, survived for longer than the revolution itself. Mayakovsky's suicide in 1930, in despair at the degeneration of the revolution, was one of the first signs that the cultural freedom inaugurated by 1917 was also coming to an end.

In music, cultural regression began with an attack on jazz, which was disparaged as a degenerate art form born of a decaying capitalism in the West. From 1929 a ban on Western jazz musicians visiting the USSR was enforced. The Soviet jazz musician Leopold Teplitsky was sent into exile. Performances of jazz were banned, and even playing jazz records could incur a fine.

In 1932, as part of a 'reorganisation' of Soviet cultural life, all independent artistic groups were shut down. Both the ASM and the RAPM were dissolved and replaced by the state-controlled Union of Soviet Composers. The tools for suppressing resistance in all spheres of Soviet life had been created. It would be another few years before the full force of state repression would be applied. When it came, Shostakovich was to find himself at the centre of the attack on the musical scene.

At the 1934 Writers' Congress, addressed by Maxim Gorky, Bukharin and the new Culture Commissar Andrei Zhdanov, a new cultural orthodoxy was introduced. Pravda reported the official definition as:

> 'Socialist realism, the basic method of Soviet artistic literature and literary criticism, demands truthfulness from the artist and an historically concrete portrayal of reality in its revolutionary development'.[2]

Of course, the definition of Socialist Realism was vacuous enough to allow the authorities to apply it with discretion to whatever art was deemed useful for the regime. The description given by Boris Asafiev, who had moved from being the champion of the avant-garde and leading light in the ASM to a Stalinist hack, was perhaps closer to the mark. He described Socialist Realism as 'an all-healing feeling of the ultimate rightness of reality'. In other words, any art that sought to challenge the official story that 'life was getting better', during the period of mass starvation caused by forced collectivisation and the bloody purge of all opposition to Stalin, was suspect.

However, there was continued resistance to the new cultural policy. At the Writers' Congress Bukharin had argued for a more sophisticated artistic policy. And in a debate at the 1935 Union of Soviet Composers' conference, Iosif Riskin put the case for:

[A] more traditionally Marxist view of art:

acknowledgment that any product of a society, whether material or cultural, reflects that society in some way, and that to force a social message onto a work of art impoverishes and demeans it.[3]

At the same conference Shostakovich criticised Socialist Realist artists for writing 'inorganic' works that offered 'trite' and 'crude' messages. Also in 1935 Gavril Popov's modernist *First Symphony* (1932) was premiered. The work was immediately banned for 'reflecting the ideology of hostile classes', but reinstated a month later after protests by Shostakovich and others.

The Nose and Lady Macbeth

I worked boldly, freely. With the enthusiasm of youth I set before myself a succession of new tasks – from instrumental works I went over to opera. It may be said, I was in a state of creative inspiration.[4]

For a time it seemed as if Shostakovich was destined for a career primarily as a composer of operas. His first work in the genre, *The Nose* (1928), was a musically extrovert take on Gogol's satire of the same name. The story is about a government official who wakes one morning to find his nose is missing. He later discovers the nose going about Moscow dressed in the uniform of a state counsellor. The nose having achieved such a high rank refuses to return to his face. There then ensues a farcical series of attempts to capture the nose as it attempts to flee. The source material was written before the revolution, and on the surface satirises the class of bourgeois civil servants. However, at a time when a new and ambitious class of bureaucrats was settling into power, Shostakovich's *The Nose* undoubtedly had a resonance, and for some an unwelcome one, for a contemporary audience. Sharp satires on this new bureaucratic class were common in the literature of the period, for example in the short stories of Ilf and Petrov and *The Master and Margarita* by Mikhail Bulgakov.

Just like his other works of the period, *The Nose* was experimental, employing atonality as well as popular style and a dizzying array of sound effects. The cacophony was too much for some. A cellist in the orchestra described how he, along with some of the audience at the first performance, ran out in horror during the entr'acte with percussion. The humour and sense of the ridiculous in the music retain their freshness even today.

In both form and style it was alone at the time in breaking from the overbearing Russian operatic tradition of Modest Mussorgsky, Tchaikovsky and Rimsky-Korsakov. This tradition was defined by a grandiose subject, and often a cloying musical sentimentality. True to form, Shostakovich broke through the stuffiness, pomposity and elitism that surrounded the operatic form. Folk music, popular ditties, sacred music, atonality and sound effects representing various bodily functions are mixed together effortlessly. *The Nose* was a true opera buffa for the 20th century.

Unfortunately, the two-year gap from composition to first performance represented a key stage in the final defeat of the revolution. By the time *The Nose* was first performed in 1930, cultural reaction was already beginning to subsume the avant-garde. The tone of the attacks in the official press was a taste of things to come:

> …an anarchist's hand-grenade…a destructive phenomenon…spreading panic across the whole front of the music theatre establishment.[5]

The Nose sank without trace and was not performed in the USSR again for over 40 years.

Shostakovich's next operatic project was enormously ambitious. Echoing Richard Wagner's monumental work *The Ring of the Nibelung* (1874), Shostakovich aimed to produce a four-opera cycle which, in his words, would deal 'with the position of women at different times in Russia'. In letters to his mother in the early 1920s, where he defended his first romantic relationship, Shostakovich clearly identified with the revolutionary ideals of free-love and sexual liberation. Certainly part of this was an attempt by a young man to justify extra-marital sex against a disapproving parent. However, the fact that all of his relationships with women, including his three marriages, involved strong, intelligent and independent people suggests a respect for women. His first marriage appeared to be a happily 'open' one. In the 1950s he expressed his conviction in favour of the right of women to an abortion at a time when abortions were illegal in the USSR.

His sympathy for the plight of women is clear in what was to be the first opera in the cycle, *Lady Macbeth of the Mtsensk District* (1932). The story is based on a 19th century book by Nikolai Leskov. It follows the saga of a woman, Katerina Izmailova, who has become locked into a loveless marriage. She takes a lover, Sergei, only after first challenging him on his womanising, and asserting that women can be every bit as strong as men. Katerina's tyrannical father-in-law, Boris, discovers her affair and savagely beats and then locks up Sergei. Katerina, in turn, kills Boris and frees Sergei. She later kills her husband, when he also discovers her affair. The lovers are caught by the police and deported to Siberia. There Sergei turns on Katerina and betrays her with another woman. Finally, and tragically Katerina kills the other woman by pushing her under the ice, whereupon Katerina herself falls in and dies too.

For sure, Katerina is no idealised heroine. With the possible exception of Boris, she murders unnecessarily and arguably without sufficient provocation to justify her actions. Yet she is a tragic character in the true sense of the word; she is locked into a series of circumstances over which she seems to have no control. And it is on that basis that Shostakovich claims our sympathy for Katerina. She is, the opera appears to say, like all women born into a society which demeans and oppresses them. Therefore her justified desire for independence, self-respect and anger towards the men in her life drives her to commit terrible acts. Katerina's tragedy is the tragedy of all women in a patriarchal society. Shostakovich described how he had altered the original story:

> [Nicolai Leskov] described Katerina as a cruel
> woman, depraved. I refused to take such a course
> and presented her as a clever woman, gifted
> and interesting... Aside from Katerina, there is
> no positive character or hero in this opera.[6]

The circumstances surrounding *Lady Macbeth* and the effect it would have on Shostakovich's career were to mirror the tragedy of its subject matter, as he became increasingly trapped in a life conditioned by fear and repression.

At first the opera was performed in Leningrad and Moscow to huge critical and popular success. In the USSR alone it was performed more than 100 times in two years. It proved a hit abroad too, staged in the year following its premiere in Cleveland, New York, Argentina, Czechoslovakia and Sweden. Then on 26 January 1936 Stalin accompanied by Molotov, Mikoyan, Zhdanov (all sitting in an armour-plated box) attended a performance in Moscow. They walked out during one of the intervals. The following day a savage attack on *Lady Macbeth*, and Shostakovich's music in general, was published in *Pravda*. Among other things, Shostakovich was accused of being a 'formalist' - someone more interested in playing with musical form and structure than in conveying a clear and simple meaning. Gorky and Shostakovich's powerful patron, Marshal Tukhachevsky, wrote to Stalin to protest against the attack. They were probably unaware that it had been written, if not by Stalin, then certainly on his orders. Meyerhold, Sollertinsky, and the composer Vissarion Shebalin all publicly supported Shostakovich. Even Prokofiev, normally keen to keep his head down, defended Shostakovich:

'What people here dub as formalism is
actually a simple matter of not understanding
something on first hearing'.[7]

If at first some believed that a debate could still be had, these hopes would be dashed when a month later another article appeared in *Pravda*, this time attacking Shostakovich's ballet *The Limpid Stream* (1935) along the same lines as 'formalist'. The anonymous article ended by warning ominously that if Shostakovich didn't change his ways 'things will turn out badly for him'. This was no idle threat. These articles appeared in 1936, the year of the first show trials and the unleashing of a bloody terror.

The experience became a crucial turning point in Shostakovich's life. The composer thrived on writing for the stage, and his two operas – *The Nose* and *Lady Macbeth* – show an outstanding talent. Yet he never completed another stage work. But the 1936 attacks on Shostakovich also represented a defining point in the history of the USSR which 'changed the Soviet cultural scene for ever'.[8]

Up until the *Lady Macbeth* furore Shostakovich had been firmly on the path of an avant-gardist. However, what had marked him out from many of the avant-garde was that he did not see artistic experimentation as necessarily counterposed to accessibility. He had been unafraid to produce challenging works such as his *Second Symphony* and *Aphorisms* (1927) for solo piano, yet at the same time produce light-hearted fare such as his variations on the popular tune 'Tea for Two', and scores for popular films.

In *Lady Macbeth* he seemed to have matched Alban Berg's achievement in Wozzeck (1925), to have produced a gripping drama, while at the same time departing from the conservatism into which the operatic form had fallen by then. In other words, Shostakovich had managed to find an artistic path which discarded the false dichotomy between 'high' and 'popular' art. As I have argued earlier, one of the major reasons Shostakovich was able to transcend this artificial divide in art was that the revolutionary impetus of socialism was driven by the desire to break down the division of labour bred by industrial capitalism, and to overcome the alienation and commercialism this produces. But as the communist ideal gave way to ruthless industrialisation and competition with the market capitalism of the West, so art in the USSR increasingly followed the same logic as that of Western capitalism. The distinction between different kinds of art, and the drive to produce mass-market populism reasserted itself firmly within Soviet culture, even if this often served a far cruder propagandistic function than in the West. In those circumstances, no matter how great a composer he was, Shostakovich would have been unable to maintain his earlier style, based as it was on the breaking down of barriers achieved by the revolution. While he continued to compose music in many different genres, *Lady Macbeth* represents his last piece to successfully incorporate such disparate forms and styles.

...the authorities tried everything they knew to get me to repent and expiate my sin. But I refused, I was young then, and had my physical strength. Instead of repenting, I wrote my *Fourth Symphony.*[1]

WHILE *LADY MACBETH* was still enjoying its huge success, Shostakovich was writing another symphonic masterpiece, his *Fourth Symphony* (1936). He was just beginning work on the last movement of the *Fourth* when the attacks on him in *Pravda* appeared. This symphony marked a new turn in Shostakovich's music, one influenced by the work of Gustav Mahler. According to Shostakovich's assistant at the time, Mahler's ambiguous and spectral *Seventh Symphony* (1905) was on his piano throughout the composition of the *Fourth Symphony.*[2] Mahler was one of Shostakovich's favourite composers. Shostakovich was inspired by Mahler's combined use of popular melodies and forms alongside strange harmonies, and his ability to convey irony in music. Mahler's music is a product of a society of extremes. Turn of the century Vienna was culturally advanced, yet politically backward. While the salons were full of high society living it up, the Austrian monarchy was decaying from within and anti-Semitism was increasingly rife. It was a society 'dancing on a volcano'. It is telling that Shostakovich should turn to such inspiration at this time. The gap between the insistent propaganda of the Stalinist dictatorship that 'life was getting better', while millions starved in the countryside, were sent to slave labour camps or summarily executed was expanding to the most perverse proportions. In the *Fourth Symphony* Shostakovich often adopts Adorno's prescription for modernist composers (which was also Adorno's description of Mahler's style) of using 'shocks' and 'disintegrations' to express the breakdown of Enlightenment ideals. One of Shostakovich's most astute biographers argues that:

> Given the political and aesthetic climate of the time [this] 'Mahlerian' work would have been construed as the epitome of formalism, an act in arrogant defiance of the Party's benevolent guidance... The symphony had been conceived on an ambitious scale, as the artistic 'credo' of an enlightened modernist; the final movement, written after the launching of the *Pravda* campaign, made no conspicuous acknowledgement of or concession to the critical furore.[3]

Pauline Fairclough, in a study of the *Fourth Symphony*, points out that it is the first composition by Shostakovich to make extensive use of allusion through musical quotations in the Mahlerian manner.[4] This was to become a stylistic trait increasingly evident in Shostakovich's work over the years. Of course, the use of allusions and metaphors allows an artist to express ideas that would otherwise fall foul of the censor. The *Fourth Symphony* echoes or quotes discretely from Tchaikovsky's *Sixth Symphony* (1893), Mahler's *Second Symphony* (1895) and Mussorgsky's *Boris Godunov* (1872).

However, in the months following the *Pravda* attacks, the *Fourth Symphony* was abruptly withdrawn during rehearsals, and would not be performed anywhere for another quarter of a century. Officially, the reason for the withdrawal was that the work was proving too difficult for the orchestra to master and that as a result Shostakovich had himself requested the cancelling of its first performance. This was highly unlikely to have been the truth. Shostakovich had written many technically challenging pieces before, and was to do so again in the future without resorting to such a drastic act of self-censorship.

According to Shostakovich's friends and family, what had happened was that during the rehearsals reports had begun to circulate that the symphony continued in the same vein as *Lady Macbeth* in pursuing an experimental and modernist path, in defiance of the diktat issued in *Pravda*. Perhaps what was of greater concern to the authorities was the highly ambiguous atmosphere generated by the work. More than any other piece by Shostakovich it plays on the style, more or less invented by Mahler, of using sharp contrasts between grotesqueness and nostalgia, between tragedy and low comedy to create a sense of alienation and of a life out of joint. And it was this unmistakable aspect of the work that almost certainly made it unacceptable to the authorities who wanted, instead, music that gave 'an all-healing feeling of the ultimate rightness of reality'.

Fifth Symphony

While the *Fourth Symphony* was shelved, Shostakovich turned instead to write his *Fifth Symphony* (1937). This symphony has proved to be his most popular work and his most enduring. Almost from the time of its premiere it achieved that rare distinction of an instant classic, becoming a central part of the repertoire of any major orchestra and conductor along with the symphonies of Beethoven and Brahms. The *Fifth Symphony* also marked Shostakovich's return to official favour and a lessening of the immediate danger of persecution. Indeed, a contemporary critic's description of the *Fifth* as a 'Soviet artist's response to just criticism' became something of an unofficial subtitle for the work.

In this one symphony Shostakovich seemed to have surmounted many of the criticisms levelled at him throughout his career; namely that he kow-towed to populism on the one hand and to political pressure on the other. How could a piece of non-vocal music express, or appear to express, all this? The answer has to do with both the form and the content of the piece. The *Fifth Symphony*, unlike all of his previous works in the genre, follows quite closely the classical structure that goes back to Haydn. It has four movements in the relatively conventional order of a sonata allegro, a scherzo followed by an adagio, and ending with a finale that brings thematic and harmonic resolution to the whole piece. In addition, the piece has many memorable themes that seem to develop naturally out of one another thus giving the piece an audible 'narrative'. The form is therefore 'conservative' in that it does not break new ground or challenge the listener in ways that some of his earlier works did. Yet anyone listening to this work would without question identify it as a work of the 20th century, which would not be the case in the symphonies of conservative composers of the time such as Erich Korngold or Edward Elgar. Shostakovich's harmonic language still retains the angularity and violence that places it unmistakably as a work of the machine age. But also there remains a Mahlerian ambiguity in the *Fifth*. This aspect of style continues to undercut whatever sense of resolution there is in the piece. There is a grotesquery that suggests something other than a simple reconciliation with, or celebration of, Stalinist society and aesthetics.

Much of the debate around this symphony has centred on its ending. Superficially, at least, it concludes triumphantly. The structure of the last movement parallels very closely the final movement of Mahler's *First Symphony* (1888). In both cases they open with the orchestra at full blast, self-consciously announcing themselves as grand finales. After a long stretch of reflection and a 'false dawn' they overcome any doubts with the orchestra marching to a glorious conclusion. However, there remains something not quite right in the closing pages of Shostakovich's *Fifth*. One musicologist argues that the conclusion deliberately reverses the tragic ending in such as a way as to make it ambiguous or unconvincing as a triumph.[5] The composer Nikolai Myaskovsky described the ending of the Fifth Symphony as 'flat' and 'empty'.[6] And yet at the same time, it can still be heard as a triumphant conclusion. At the premiere of the piece on 21 November 1937 the audience began to stand up and applaud even before the music had died out. Mikhail Chulaki, Director of Leningrad Philharmonic, described the reactions of government officials to the symphony:

> It was simple in language, was full of extended melodies, and what was most important, it finished with victorious fanfares whose "outspoken" nature could not be called into doubt.[7]

As Shostakovich wryly noted to the conductor Boris Khaikin in late 1937:

> I finished the *Fifth Symphony* in the major and fortissimo…It would be interesting to know what would have been said if I finished it pianissimo and in the minor.[8]

However, there must have been some among the ruling circles who recognised and remained anxious about the ambiguity of the symphony's 'message'. A special performance was arranged for leading Communist Party officials. It was only after this performance that the party officially designated the symphony as an 'optimistic tragedy'. In performance, the *Fifth* appears to defy attempts to define it as triumphant, tragic or terrifying, as is evident when listening to recordings of vastly different interpretations of the finale by various conductors; Leonard Bernstein and Mstislav Rostropovich, in their recordings, create diametrically opposed interpretations, yet both remain musically 'valid' and faithful to the score. Perhaps the whole point of the symphony is that it expresses the schizoid atmosphere of Russia in 1937, a society in which Stalin was proudly claiming the triumph of 'socialism in one country' and the country's economy was modernising at a fantastic rate, while at the same time there was mass starvation in the countryside and the purges were devouring by the thousands the last living links to the revolution of 1917.

With the horrors of Stalinism reaching an apogee, and a growing realisation that the liberating air of the revolution had been definitively sucked out of Soviet society, the *Fifth Symphony* represents Shostakovich's first in a line of symphonies (*Fifth, Seventh, Eighth, Twelfth*) which adopted a narrative or style in keeping with the demands of Socialist Realism, yet maintained enough ambiguity in terms of meaning which allowed veiled critiques of Stalinism to be made or understood by the audience. These works contrast with symphonies such as his *Second, Thirteenth and Fourteenth* which employ far more ambiguity of tonality and form, yet convey a clear 'message'. What Shostakovich proved in practice was that in an art form as abstract as music, it is possible to exploit the unstable relationship between form and content in a way which can express at the *same time* the truths and falsehoods of life in an alienated society. What makes this mode of expression so powerful is precisely the fact that we experience the struggle between understanding what is true, and what is not true about ourselves and our society every day. In this Shostakovich was truly following in the footsteps of his hero, Mahler, who democratised musical language not by making it 'easy' or populist, but by finding a way to make his music engage with what Sollertinsky described as a 'collective consciousness'.

The Soviet philosopher of language Mikhail Bakhtin's 'dialogical' principle, developed in the 1930s, makes the audience as much a part in creating meaning as the author.[9] Bakhtin argued that a text could contain many different voices and was itself part of an ongoing dialogue between genre, language, art, audience, culture and society, thus allowing for varying interpretations to be made of the work. In discussing literature, Bakhtin allowed for significant authorial control over meaning through the manner in which the story is told. However, if we apply the same principle to music the audience has even more autonomy from the author than in literature, due to the increased abstraction of the musical form.[10] Bakhtin thus offers a useful corrective to Adorno's often elitist analysis of the relationship between the artist and the audience. For Adorno, late capitalism had created an audience seduced by commercialism, who needed to be shocked by the composer (who has somehow escaped from this stupefied state) into an awareness of reality.[11] Rather than the audience being the mere recipient of meaning, the interpretation of music is 'socially negotiated'[12] between composer, performer and audience. I would argue that

Shostakovich's music has been more the subject of 'social negotiation' than any other 20th century composer. This explains both the seemingly endless debates over the meanings, musical and political, of his works and his ability to engage a large popular audience with his music. But the extent of the social negotiation with Shostakovich's music was only possible because he himself was so committed to communicating with a mass audience, without falling into the trap of patronising them with populist banalities.

It would be wrong to suggest that Shostakovich's temporary return to official favour following the *Fifth Symphony* had removed any danger to himself or his family. Among the victims of the terror during 1937 was the civil war hero Mikhail Tukhachevsky who had been a supporter and patron of Shostakovich since 1925. Indeed, in the days following Tukhachevsky's arrest, the musicologist and friend of Shostakovich, Nikolai Khilyaev, was arrested on the basis of his connections with Tukhachevsky. Around the same time Shostakovich was summoned to NKVD (the secret police) headquarters. His interrogator asked Shostakovich if he had heard Tukhachevsky discussing a plan to assassinate Stalin. When Shostakovich replied that he had never heard him discuss anything of the sort, the NKVD officer told him to 'remember' and come back again a few days later. When Shostakovich returned at the appointed time, convinced that he was about to be arrested, he was told that his interrogator had himself been arrested, thus leaving Shostakovich free to go home.

In the same year Shostakovich's brother-in-law, the physicist Vsevolod Fredericks, was arrested and sent to a slave labour camp. Shostakovich's elder sister was sent into exile, while his mother-in-law was arrested and sent to the camps. His friend the Marxist writer

Galina Serebryakova was also arrested and condemned to slave labour. Shostakovich's uncle, the Old Bolshevik Maxim Kostrykin, died in the camps, as did the poet Boris Kornilov, author of the text to Shostakovich's hit *Song of the Counterplan* along with Adrian Piotrovsky, Shostakovich's collaborator on *The Limpid Stream*. And in 1939 Meyerhold was also arrested and shot, while Meyerhold's wife died in mysterious circumstances. The strain on Shostakovich must have been unbearable. He took to keeping a packed suitcase by his front door, in readiness for the arrival of Stalin's secret police. The Stalinist terror only seemed to subside with the onslaught of an even greater terror with the Nazi invasion of 1941.

Shostakovich: Socialism, Stalin & Symphonies

WHILE SOME HAVE ATTEMPTED to equate the Stalinist dictatorship with the Nazis, it was clear to many Russians at the time, including Shostakovich, that Hitler's regime was qualitatively worse than Stalin's. In no way does this downplay the horrors of Stalinism. Rather, the difference was between an ideology which saw mass murder as a justifiable means to an end (Stalinism), and a belief in genocide as an end in itself (Nazism). For this reason, millions of Russians courageously rallied to the defence against the Nazi invasion in spite of and not because of Stalin.

Culturally, the war allowed a space for the expression of terror, despair and resistance against tyranny. Throughout the 1930s all these things had been a reality of everyday life, but had remained obscured by the veil of cultural censorship that was Socialist Realism. It was considered treachery to express these things when official propaganda was promoting the successful building of 'socialism in one country'. But with the USSR in grave peril at the hands of the Nazi threat, it became possible to express a much broader range of emotions. But of course, it can be impossible to distinguish in abstract art precisely against what one is expressing horror or resistance. Many

Russians at the time understood, or chose to find in cultural works of the period, expressions of horror and resistance towards both the Nazis and Stalinism.

Shostakovich and his wartime works, perhaps more than any other Soviet artist of the time came to embody the duality and ambiguity that became possible during this period. On the one hand he was celebrated by the Soviet regime and its allies as a loyal and courageous defender of the USSR. Shostakovich was photographed in a fireman's uniform helping to defend Leningrad under siege. This image was extensively used for propaganda purposes by the Soviet government, and was reproduced on the front cover of *Time* magazine as part of a drive to build support for bringing the USA into the war.

The image of Shostakovich as an emblem of Soviet resistance was cemented with his *Seventh Symphony* (1941). with the subtitle the 'Leningrad', Shostakovich began writing it during the siege of the city. Work on the symphony was interrupted by his evacuation to Kuibyshev in the autumn of 1941. Shostakovich wrote to a friend that 'as soon as I got on that train, something snapped inside me... I can't compose just now, knowing how many people are losing their lives.' Shostakovich, along with the rest of the Soviet Union, seemed to breathe a small sigh of relief when the Nazis advance was stopped at Moscow, and he finished the symphony in the space of a few weeks.

The story of the *Seventh Symphony's* first performances involves a combination of heroic stoicism under extraordinary conditions, a wartime drama of derring-do, and a soap opera involving two of the musical titans of the age. The symphony's world premiere took place in conditions a world away from red carpets and grand concert halls. Instead it was performed by a smallish orchestra made up of musicians cobbled together at short notice, in a provincial town used as a retreat from the war's front line. Following this, the score was copied onto microfilm and sent via Tehran to the USA. The chance to be the first to conduct the symphony outside of Russia became a turf war between two megalomaniac conductors, Arturo Toscanini and Leopold Stokowski. Toscanini, being far and away the more ruthless of the two, triumphed and his performance of the symphony was broadcast live to millions of Americans.

The real point about all this drama surrounding the *Seventh Symphony* is the extent to which a piece of classical music, moreover a complex work lasting for over an hour, achieved such prestige and fame among millions of people across the world. Part of the reason was that the work's reputation was inflated as part of a massive propaganda effort by the wartime allies. Famously, the opening movement contains a 15 minute long march theme in which Shostakovich employed Ravel's technique in *Bolero* (1928) of development through repetition and a gradually building orchestration. This march no doubt guaranteed a certain level of popularity solely due to the excitement of its visceral evocation of an invading army brutalising everything in its wake.

Many people have dismissed the 'invasion theme' as banal (Bartok satirised it in his *Concerto for Orchestra* [1943]) or as a piece of populist programme music. But I can't think of any other piece of classical music which so vividly captures the feeling of terror of an approaching army on the march. Moreover, the 'invasion theme' has a context within the symphony which gives it a greater power and sophistication than it possesses of its own accord. First, the theme ends not in a programmatic way, or in apotheosis as in the case of *Bolero*, but rather the music collapses into itself in a manner that suggests some kind of open-mouthed horror. The movement ends not with a bang but a whimper. And in many ways the heart of the symphony is not in this famous first movement, but rather in the succeeding three movements which conjure up deep longing for a life without war, and nostalgia for life's small joys. Shostakovich described the slow movement as an evocation of the 'white nights' of Leningrad summers when people partied late into the night.

But again there is an ambiguity to the music. Flora Litvinova, daughter-in-law of Maxim Litvinov, Soviet foreign minister until 1939, recalled Shostakovich telling her that the brutality described in the *Seventh's* first movement was not just about fascism but about the Stalinist terror too. In his second wartime symphony, the *Eighth* (1943), Shostakovich leaves behind the C-Major resoluteness of the *Seventh* and employs instead its parallel key, C-Minor. The significance of Shostakovich using C-Minor is two-fold. It marked his return to this key for the first time since the modernist masterpieces the *Concerto for Piano, Trumpet and Strings* (1933) and the *Fourth Symphony* (1935), suggesting a conscious attempt to exploit the more artistically relaxed war years to return to a more adventurous style. In addition, C-Minor is the key of Beethoven's *Fifth Symphony* (1808) as well as his *Third Piano Concerto* (1801) and *'Pathetique' Sonata* (1798), Mahler's *Second Symphony* (1895) and one of Chopin's *Nocturnes* (1841). All of these pieces share an emotionally unstable character as well as a sense of great struggle against adversity, always teetering on the verge of tragedy. Following in this tradition of C-Minor pieces, Shostakovich's *Eighth Symphony* was too ambiguous and lacking in uncomplicated heroism for the liking of the Soviet authorities. Due to the all-consuming focus on defeating the Nazis, the symphony was merely frowned upon rather than attacked by Soviet officials. But the strange and spectral mood of much of the piece, along with a scherzo of enormous motoric energy and venomous attack, makes the *Eighth Symphony* one of Shostakovich's most compelling works.

Resistance

Following the defeat of Nazi Germany, Shostakovich had an opportunity to cement the high prestige in official circles that he had won with his wartime 'patriotic' works. But bravely, he resisted the temptation to become a 'court composer' for Stalin. The Soviet government commissioned from him his *Ninth Symphony* (1945). Ever since Beethoven's *Ninth*, a celebration of the revolutionary ideals of the Enlightenment, the ninth symphony of a composer has raised expectations for some sort of grand apotheosis. Thus, it was expected of Shostakovich that his *Ninth Symphony* would be a stirring epic, celebrating victory in the 'Great Patriotic War'. The official Soviet news agency, TASS reported in the summer of 1945 that Shostakovich was working on a new symphony 'Devoted to the Celebration of our Great Victory'. The press began trailing rumours that Shostakovich was going to produce his long-awaited 'Lenin' symphony, and no doubt Stalin expected some form of praise to himself, as had become almost, required by etiquette in major public works of art at this time.

Instead Shostakovich produced a symphony that could not be further from such expectations. The *Ninth Symphony*, premiered in November 1945, is classical in form with a lightness of style suggestive of whimsicalness. The first movement includes a satirical march featuring that most pompous-sounding of instruments, the bassoon. No attempt at ascertaining the 'real' meaning of this symphony is necessary here. It quite obviously cut against the grain of what was expected, and this was not lost on the government officials who had commissioned it. Once again Shostakovich was attacked in the official press, and his attitude considered suspect.

Jewish music

However much his *Ninth Symphony* displeased the dictatorship, it contains nothing that could be considered overtly political. It can easily be seen in the tradition of a 'fool's joke'. What might have worried the authorities more was his persistence in pursuing uncomfortable themes and musical styles in his chamber works. The *Third String Quartet* (1946) was roundly condemned for its pessimistic and ambiguous tone. Shostakovich's *Second Piano Trio* (1944), dedicated to his closest friend, Sollertinsky, who had recently died, was the first of many works that included Jewish folk style and quotations from Jewish folk songs. The *Second Piano Trio* was also written contemporaneously with Vasily Grossman's famous reports in the Soviet press, which gave the first harrowing descriptions of Nazi death camps in Poland. In a country in which anti-Semitism was rife this was a clear statement of Shostakovich's lifelong anti-racism.

Shostakovich continued to pursue Jewish themes in his music during what became known as the 'Doctors' Plot'. This was, like the accusations of a 'Trotskyite/Fascist' threat in the 1930s, a completely fabricated story used to justify another round of purges and repression. But this time the narrative had even nastier overtones directed at

Jews, who were supposedly behind a plot by doctors to poison leading Soviet bureaucrats. It was also well known that in many parts of the USSR, people had collaborated with the Nazi invaders in persecuting Jews. In 1947 Shostakovich again included Jewish themes in his *First Violin Concerto*. And in 1948 he produced a song cycle *From Jewish Folk Poetry*. Shostakovich must have known he was skating on thin ice.

Zhdanovshina

Fearful that the chaos of the war had allowed the bonds of artistic censorship to slacken too much, the Soviet government began to restore a stricter regime. Stalin appointed one of his inner circle, Andrei Zhdanov, as his cultural commissar. Zhdanov began a series of attacks on the various arts in order to reimpose ideological conformity. Following attacks in 1946 on leading writers such as Anna Akhmatova and Shostakovich's close friend Mikhail Zoshchenko, Zhdanov moved on to the cinema and theatre. In music the attacks followed a similar pattern to those of 1936. The day after Stalin attended Vano Muradeli's opera *The Great Friendship* in January 1948, Zhdanov convened a Congress of the Composers' Union. In fact, Muradeli's work was a piece of Socialist Realist hackwork, which had inadvertently offended Stalin by, among other things, rearranging Stalin's favourite folk tune. However, for Stalin and his cohort, this simply provided a useful pretext for stamping out any independence among musicians.

The remit of the Congress was clear: to put the USSR's leading modernist composers in their place, and reassert the policy of Socialist Realism. Zhdanov read out the charges, now familiar through repetition, of 'formalism' and 'anti-people' tendencies. The ferocity of the attack is summed up by Zhdanov's description of the works of Shostakovich and his fellow modernists as 'musical gas-chambers'. Shostakovich was the focus of repeated denunciations not just from Zhdanov, but also in speech after speech from mediocre composers, either jealous of his talent or jockeying for position with the regime. As Shostakovich went to the rostrum to speak in his own defence, he was handed a prepared speech by one of the union officials and ordered to deliver it. At one point he broke away from the text and said:

> It always seems to me that when I write sincerely and as I truly feel, then my music cannot be 'against' the people, after all I myself am a representative...in some small way...of the people.[1]

Shostakovich concluded, 'I suppose instructions will now be given.' This was a clear verbal expression of the sardonic pessimism that increasingly came to feature in his music over the following years. It was about this time that Shostakovich began work on a piece of music, written for his own private amusement, the *Anti-Formalist Rayok* (1948). The Russian word 'rayok' can be variously translated as 'little paradise', 'peepshow' or 'rhyming patter', but in this context it refers to a raucously satirical work – imagine an extended dramatic limerick crossed with elements of pantomime. Mussorgsky, one of Shostakovich's favourite composers, had written a satirical piece entitled *Rayok* (1870) attacking the musical and political philistines of his day. Shostakovich's version satirises the 1948 'anti-formalist' campaign. Among other things it takes the piss out of Stalin's favourite folk song, and sends up Zhdanov's embarrassing mispronunciation of the name of Rimsky-Korsakov at the Union of Composers Congress that year. Another piece written many years later, entitled *Preface to the Complete Collection of My Works and Brief Reflections on this Preface* (1966), is another satirical work in the same vain, which ridicules the long list of honours and awards heaped upon him during his career. Needless to say, neither of these works were intended for publication, and they did not receive public performances until years after his death. But they do offer a glimpse of the biting sarcastic humour, testified to by many of his closest friends, which grew over the years into an increasing bitterness about Soviet life in general, and his treatment by the authorities in particular.

On 10 February the Central Committee issued the decree 'On V Muradeli's opera *The Great Friendship*'. The six composers named and shamed in the Decree were Shostakovich, Sergei Prokofiev, Aram Khachaturian, Vissarion Shebalin, Gavril Popov, and Nicolai Myaskovsky; a veritable roll-call of the greatest living Soviet composers of that time. In the months following the decree, further attacks on Shostakovich appeared in *Pravda*. He was sacked from his teaching posts, and all his works, except for the *Fifth* and *Seventh* symphonies, were banned. Shostakovich's young son, Maxim, was temporarily withdrawn from his music school for fear that the attacks initiated by the decree would also affect him.

Retreat

The situation for Shostakovich must have seemed bleak. Still only in his early forties and with a young family to support, he was forced into a series of humiliating acts. In early spring 1949 Stalin phoned Shostakovich personally and asked him to represent the USSR at the World Congress of Peace and Culture in New York. Shostakovich told

Stalin it would be awkward because most of his works were banned. Stalin's obviously disingenuous reply was 'Forbidden by whom? What do you mean forbidden?' A few days later an official order signed by Stalin revoked the ban on Shostakovich's works that had been in place since the decree a year earlier. Although the trip to New York was not a happy one for Shostakovich, it demonstrated the enormous international popularity of his music. Aaron Copland, Norman Mailer and Arthur Miller as well as several thousand musicians welcomed him at the airport. The US press release reported the USSR delegation to the Congress as 'Dmitri Shostakovich and accompanying persons'.

Back in the USSR Shostakovich, deprived of teaching work, produced public compositions of abject servility purely as a means of supporting himself and his family. His oratorio *The Song of the Forests* (1949) hailed Stalin as the great leader and teacher of the people, and he wrote the film score for *The Unforgettable 1919* (1951), which rewrote history to suggest that Stalin, rather than Trotsky, had been the leading strategist in the defence of the revolution during the civil war. Yet in private Shostakovich continued to write music of great feeling and artistic integrity. These included his *Fourth* (1949) and *Fifth* (1952) string quartets, and the *Twenty Four Preludes and Fugues* (1950) for piano. But in these works he seemed to move away from expressing larger themes in favour of more personal or purely musical ideas. Shostakovich would never completely stop writing great music, but increasingly the zest for life, the musical eclecticism and engagement with the big social issues of the day began to disappear from his music. Shostakovich himself began to cut a more withdrawn figure and to appear ever more guarded and contradictory in his public statements.

Shostakovich watching his beloved soccer team Zenit Leningrad.

Miraculously luminous,
Light splintering through a myriad of facets,
It alone speaks to me.

While all others dared not approach,
And the ultimate companion averted his eyes,
It stayed with me in my grave,
Singing like the first summer storm,
Or did all the flowers speak at the same time.

Music by Anna Akhmatova (dedicated to Shostakovich)

ON 13 JANUARY 1953 THE Soviet press reported the arrests of 'saboteur doctors' who had allegedly been spreading plague and other infections. Seven of the nine doctors arrested were Jews. This was the signal for a new purge, perhaps one to rival in violence and ruthlessness those of the 1930s, only this time coloured by anti-Semitism. Luckily in March 1953, just as the 'Doctors' Plot' and the purges that were to accompany it were gathering pace, fate intervened and Stalin died. Perhaps realising that the Soviet ruling class had achieved through massive industrialisation and the post-war conquest of Eastern Europe a level of stability which would be jeopardised by renewed purges, the ruling Presidium moved swiftly following Stalin's death to halt the momentum for a new round of bloodletting. The most hard-nosed Stalinist remaining in the leadership, the brutal chief of the secret police Lavrenti Beria was arrested and shot. Other allies of Stalin such as Molotov were simply removed from office. The mood of the new leadership was already apparent during Stalin's lying in state. The great violinist David Oistrakh was playing suitably sombre music at the Hall of Columns where Stalin's body was on display to the public. During a brief rest Nikita Khrushchev, smiling broadly, asked Oistrakh to play something more cheerful.[1]

Immediately following Stalin's death and for the first time in over five years, Shostakovich produced a major public work of originality and independence. His *Tenth Symphony* (1953) is considered by many to be Shostakovich's crowning masterpiece and to represent the very high point of his symphonic works. According to dubious evidence in *Testimony*, the second movement, a wild scherzo, is supposed to represent Stalin. Whether it does or not, it certainly evokes a sense of evil and frenzy which it would have been hard to have publicly performed in the preceding years. But the symphony is also evidence of a growing introversion in his music. Much of the music is built on a four-note motif, D-S-C-H, the composer's initials.[2] In addition, the third movement, a nocturne, uses the DSCH motif as well as another, even more obscure, motif made up of the initials of the name of a student of his, with whom he seems to have been infatuated at the time. In early 1954 a Composers' Union conference was convened to discuss the *Tenth Symphony*. It was condemned as 'pessimistic', 'gloomy' and 'modernist'. It would take time before the 'Thaw' following Stalin's death would make its full effects felt in Soviet life. But already the political climate had relaxed, and the criticisms this time did not presage any further attacks on Shostakovich or the musical scene generally.

For about three years immediately following the composition of the *Tenth Symphony* Shostakovich experienced something of an artistic crisis. He had always been an enormously prolific composer yet from 1954 to 1956 he composed very little, mostly film scores and a few songs. Why this was the case can only be a matter of speculation. Shostakovich thought he had written himself out. In other words he was experiencing a form of writer's block. My own feeling is that it was partly a result of difficult personal circumstances with the sudden death of his wife in 1954 followed by an unhappy and short-lived second marriage. But also it is possible that it was difficult for him to compose fluently again after five years of severe censorship for the second time in his life.

In addition, it might have been difficult for him to adjust to such a different social context. Throughout his career, from his teens onwards, the fortunes of the revolution had played a central role in his work. The feeling of struggle, of tragedy and of fear that he had so successfully honed in his work enabled him, more than any other Soviet composer, to express the violent and conflicting emotions wrought by the Nazi invasion. However, in the initial period following Stalin's death, and with the Soviet leadership confused and hesitant as to what strategy to pursue, a period of political and social stagnation ensued. As bound up as Shostakovich had been with the social and political concerns of his era, I think it is highly likely that he felt equally confused and disorientated during this period, and this fed into a lack of focus in composition.

Renewed hopes and a return to form

The interregnum following Stalin's death came to an end in 1956. In February of that year Nikita Khrushchev, who had emerged victorious from the power struggle to succeed Stalin, made his famous 'secret speech' to the 20th Congress of the Soviet Communist Party in which he denounced Stalin. This began a process of political liberalisation. Hundreds of thousands were released from the gulags, victims of the purges were 'rehabilitated' and there was an end to the incessant bloodshed of the Stalin period. In cultural life censorship was relaxed; this was a period which would see the official publication of Aleksandr Solzhenitsyn's novella of life in the gulag, *One Day in the Life of Ivan Denisovich*.

In 1956 Shostakovich's compositional ability appeared to experience a rehabilitation too. That year saw him compose his *Sixth String Quartet* and his *Second Piano Concerto*, both good if not exceptional works. He had planned to write a symphony in 1995 to mark the 50th anniversary of the 1905 Revolution, but had been unable to complete it. Finally, in 1957 he produced his *Eleventh Symphony* subtitled '1905'. Lasting over an hour with four movements following one after the other without a break, it demonstrates Shostakovich's remarkable grasp of symphonic form. It has been argued that the *Eleventh* is nothing more than a score in search of a film, suggesting that it is banal or populist. For the first time Shostakovich gave each movement a programmatic title: 'The Palace Square', '9th January', 'In Memoriam' and 'Alarm'. From the opening sombre evocation of a gathering demonstration to the 'rat-a-tat' percussion of the Cossacks firing on the demonstrators on 'Bloody Sunday' the music conjures up many vivid images. But it maintains enough of a self-contained musical structure for it to be a gripping piece of music on its own, which a film score cannot do over a similar span of time.

Unsurprisingly, many commentators who wish to pigeon-hole Shostakovich as an anti-Communist dissident have struggled to explain the *Eleventh Symphony*. It has been suggested that it is really a veiled description of the failed uprising in Hungary in the autumn of 1956. Indeed, one reliable source has Shostakovich saying as much to Igor Belsky, a choreographer who set the *Eleventh Symphony* as ballet. Belsky was told by Shostakovich, 'Don't forget that I wrote that symphony in the aftermath of the Hungarian Uprising'.[1] Writing the symphony in the months following the Soviet invasion of Hungary no doubt created a parallel in Shostakovich's mind of defenceless civilians facing repression by a brutal dictatorship. And it is possible to suppose that he intended the symphony to have the veiled meaning that others ascribe to it. But equally it is simplistic and flying in the face of certain facts to describe the *Eleventh* as an anti-communist work.

It was also possible that Shostakovich saw himself as anti-Stalinist yet pro-communist, or at least as a defender of the revolution. Indeed, Stalinism was built on the corpses of the many thousands of dedicated communists who saw Stalinism as the negation and not the continuation of the revolution. If Shostakovich wanted to write a straightforwardly anti-communist piece about the suppression of the Hungarian revolution, why give it a title that at the very least invites identification of it as a pro-communist work. He could, as with seven of his ten previous symphonies, have given the work no subtitle at all. It seems far more likely that like many others on the left, in both the East and West, he saw the Soviet invasion of Hungary as a betrayal of communist ideals, and wished to suggest parallels between the old Tsarist regime and the Stalinist dictatorship. Possibly as he was already planning the symphony before the events in Hungary, the uprising gave him a renewed inspiration to finally complete it in order to remind his audience of the ideals of the Russian revolution, which had been so corrupted by those who claimed to act in its name. Moreover, the fact that this was the first time since the early 1930s that he had written a major work on the subject of the revolution cannot be easily dismissed. When one considers that it was followed a few years later by the *Twelfth Symphony* (1961), dedicated to Lenin and the revolution of 1917, it seems likely that Shostakovich had a sincere belief, along with many others at the time, that the Khrushchev 'thaw' would begin to restore the USSR to what it was prior to Stalin's rule.

Eighth Quartet

One day in the summer of 1960 Shostakovich told his daughter Galina that he had just finished writing a piece dedicated to his own memory. This is confirmed in a letter he wrote to his friend Isaac Glikman:

> As hard as I tried to rough out the film scores which I am supposed to be doing, I still haven't managed to get anywhere; instead I wrote this ideologically flawed quartet which is of no use to anybody. I started thinking that if some day I die, nobody is likely to write a work in memory of me, so I had better write one myself. The title page could carry the dedication: 'To the memory of the composer of this quartet'.[4]

The piece to which he referred was the *Eighth String Quartet*, undoubtedly a masterpiece, and arguably a work that ranks alongside such classics of the genre as Beethoven's late *String Quartets*. In my opinion what makes the *Eighth String Quartet* such a great work is the way in which Shostakovich achieves a synthesis between themes of a deeply personal nature, while at the same time he gives voice to the tragedies of the age. Once again he employed the DSCH motif in a variety of inventive ways. Also included are quotations from his *First* and *Eighth* symphonies, *Second Piano Trio*, *First Cello Concerto* and *Lady Macbeth*. From other composers he alludes to Wagner's *Funeral March* from *Götterdämmerung*, Tchaikovsky's *Sixth Symphony* and the revolutionary song *Tormented by Grievous Bondage* (reputedly Lenin's favourite). Apart from his own *First Symphony,* what all these pieces have in common is their tragic quality of death and mourning. The inclusion of the *First Symphony* no doubt reflects his own mourning for a lost youth, and perhaps also a lost society. Also he was, at this time, having to cope with the onset of a debilitating and degenerative, yet still undiagnosed, disease.

But publicly he stated that he had written the piece during a stay in Dresden, a city that had been destroyed by Allied bombing during the war. The main purpose of his visit was to write the score for *Five Days, Five Nights* (1960), a film about the wartime destruction of the city. The official dedication of the work is to 'the victims of fascism and war'. Arguments have been traded back and forth about whether the quartet is what its official dedication states, whether it is in fact really a requiem for the victims of Stalinism or purely autobiographical. This attempt to say that the quartet must be just one or the other demeans it as the masterpiece it is: part of its greatness is that it is able to incorporate elements of all three. He was able to link his own personal tragedy with the wider tragedy of a society that had experienced the horrors of Stalinism, fascism and war.

The piece itself is in the key of C-Minor. It contains five movements linked together without a break. The DSCH motif is at the heart of every movement, which points to a dominant autobiographical theme. The quartet has a sombre opening movement. This is followed by a frenzied, brutalist second movement which is only relieved at the end by the main Jewish theme from his *Second Piano Trio*. The fourth movement opens with *Tormented by Grievous Bondage* immediately followed by a theme of betrayal from *Lady Macbeth,* an opera still banned at the time. The coupling of a classic revolutionary tune with a theme of betrayal invites us to at least consider that Shostakovich believed not that the revolution was wrong, but that its betrayal by those who banned *Lady Macbeth* was the real crime. The concluding movement breaks down in a way that is heartbreaking, with the last chord dying away while resisting its own demise. The *Eighth String Quartet* is a piece that demands the listener's attention and contemplation. And it should be mentioned that Shostakovich is able to achieve all of this in a piece that lasts barely twenty minutes.

The rehabilitation of Lady Macbeth

The Khrushchev 'thaw' extended to the musical scene on 28 May 1958 when the decree of 1948 was officially 'corrected', effectively lifting the ban on all works and composers imposed a decade earlier. Just two years earlier a committee of musicians representing the Composers' Union, including Dmitri Kabalevsky, visited Shostakovich to discuss the possible rehabilitation of *Lady Macbeth*. Shostakovich played the whole score through for them on the piano. When he had finished they 'pounced' on him, referring to the *Pravda* article of 1936 and the 1948 decree. Having had his hopes raised, Shostakovich was devastated when the committee refused permission for the opera to be restaged.

However, following the revocation of the 1948 decree, Shostakovich was once again invited to perform the opera, now renamed *Katerina Ismailova*, for the leaders of the Composers' Union. But this time Tikhon Khrennikov, secretary of the union and one of Shostakovich's chief persecutors in 1948, said immediately after the performance:

> This work represents the best musical memory of our youth. All of us have tolerated too much error and injustice.[5]

In early 1963 *Katerina Ismailova* was finally restaged in the USSR for the first time in almost thirty years. Once again it proved a hit with audiences. In three different productions it was staged over the following two years in Leningrad, Moscow, Kazan, Kiev and Riga. Abroad the opera was revived in Zagreb, at Covent Garden in London, at the Staatsoper in Vienna and at La Scala Milan. And in 1966 a film version was made in the USSR.

Perhaps the crowning event in this rehabilitation of Shostakovich's early works was the premiere, also in 1963 and three decades after its composition, of his *Fourth Symphony*. A few weeks after its first performance in the USSR, the *Fourth* was the centrepiece of a large retrospective of his works at the Edinburgh Festival. And it was during this period that Shostakovich was showered with the most prestigious artistic prizes in Europe: made an honorary member of the Accademia di Santa Cecilia in Rome and the Royal Academy of Music in London; made a Commandeur de l'Ordre des Arts et des Lettres in France; awarded an Honorary Doctorate from Oxford University and the Sibelius Prize, becoming its third recipient after Stravinsky and Hindemith. And at home Shostakovich received the dubious honour of being admitted to membership of the Communist Party and appointed a Deputy to the Supreme Soviet.

Shostakovich and the new generation

Shostakovich was also allowed back to teach at his alma mater, the Leningrad Conservatoire. One of the important consequences of the 'correction' of the 1948 decree was to allow the beginnings of a new Soviet avant-garde. This included young composers such as Alfred Schnittke, Sofia Gubaidulina, Edison Denisov, Boris Tchaikovsky and Boris Tischenko, all of whom were either students of Shostakovich at the Conservatoire or inspired by his music. Gubaidulina has described the impact of his work:

> Shostakovich's music reaches such a wide audience because he was able to transform the pain that he so keenly experienced into something exalted and full of light, which transcends all worldly suffering. He was able to transfigure the material into a spiritual entity, whereas Prokofiev's music lacks the contrast between terrible darkness and an ever-expanding light. We listened to Shostakovich's new works in a kind of exaltation. His concerts were events not only of musical but of political significance.'[6]

Indeed, the extent of Shostakovich's influence is evident in the frequent echoes of his distinctive style in many of these younger composers' music. In particular, Schnittke's development of 'polystylism' owes a great deal, as he willingly acknowledged, to the uninhibited eclecticism of Shostakovich's works from the 1920s and early 1930s.

On the other hand, there was a certain distance between Shostakovich and many of the new avant-garde. This was not principally to do with the gap in age. This younger generation had no direct experience of the revolutionary years of the 1920s. Instead they had been born and brought up during Stalin's dictatorship, which has sought to claim the revolution as its heritage. This meant that, unlike Shostakovich, these younger composers tended to be hostile to the whole revolutionary tradition, with some of them like Gubaidulina and Schnittke turning to religious belief as a form of resistance.

There was also a key distinction between the avant-garde of the 1920s which had formed Shostakovich and that of the 1950s. Schoenberg, Stravinsky and Shostakovich all saw what they were doing as both a continuation of as well as a break with the classical tradition which they had inherited. By contrast the avant-garde of the post-war period, led by Pierre Boulez and Karlheinz Stockhausen, saw their mission in terms of completely dispensing with the classical tradition, which they regarded as outdated and corrupted by its association with the inter-war dictatorships. This radical change in outlook, between Shostakovich's generation of modernists and the generation which came after 1945, represents a severe and perhaps irreparable rupture in the classical tradition.[7] Most composers of Shostakovich's generation found it impossible to relate to the new avant-garde. It says much for him, that along with Stravinsky, Shostakovich was one of the very few who were able to relate to and inspire this new generation of composers.

Thirteenth Symphony

With the avowedly pro-communist *Eleventh* and *Twelfth* symphonies, and the relative cultural liberalisation of the Khrushchev government Shostakovich was firmly back in official favour, and widely acknowledged as the pre-eminent living Soviet composer. But just as he did immediately following World War II, he used whatever political capital he had to assert his artistic independence. His *Thirteenth Symphony* (1962) is yet another masterpiece which demonstrates a shift toward experimenting with changes to symphonic form and more challenging harmonies. The *Thirteenth* was also the closest Shostakovich ever came to openly challenging the dictatorship. It is striking that he does this by explicitly invoking the revolution and communist ideas rather than rejecting them. It is possible to identify the *Thirteenth* as the last in a trilogy of symphonies which deal with the history of the Russian revolution from its 'dress rehearsal' in 1905 (*Eleventh Symphony*), to its triumph (*Twelfth Symphony*) to its betrayal (*Thirteenth Symphony*).

The *Thirteenth* is set to a selection of poems by Yevgeny Yevtushenko. The first, and the one that gives the symphony its subtitle, is 'Babi Yar'. This poem was published as part of the 'T.haw' in September 1961 in the same journal that a year later would publish *One Day in the Life of Ivan Denisovich*. The poem alludes to the massacre by the Nazis of over 100,000 men, women and children, most of whom were Jews, at a ravine near Kiev in 1941. But the heart of the text is an unambiguous condemnation of Russian anti-Semitism. The line 'Let the "International" thunder out when the last anti-Semite on the earth has finally been buried' seeks to draw a clear red line between the ideals of communism and a racism which the 'Communist' regime had exploited ever since the 'Doctors' Plot'. Another of the poems set by Shostakovich, *Fears,* speaks openly of the experiences of repression during the Stalin period. Indeed, Fears was the only poem from the cycle used by Shostakovich which he had specially commissioned from Yevtushenko for the symphony. The opening of the Fears movement marks Shostakovich's first use of Schoenberg's serial techniques, a device particularly suited to expressing a feeling of alienation. Yevtushenko paid tribute many years later to what working with Shostakovich had meant to him:

> [He] changed me as a poet... It was a great school of composition because Shostakovich proved that there are no elements in art that cannot be put together. One must be brave and try to unite what seems to be incompatible.[8]

Unsurprisingly, the Soviet authorities insisted on changes to the text to obscure the focus on anti-Semitism, and to blunt the radical edge of the poems. Yevtushenko, under pressure, made the changes but in an act of real bravery the original text was used for the work's premiere in December 1962. The political tensions surrounding the performance were quite extraordinary. Not one but two bass soloists required for the work dropped out under direct political pressure from the government. The conductor, Yevgeny Mravinsky, who had premiered almost every one of Shostakovich's symphonies since the *Fifth* in 1937, also dropped out shortly before the first performance. And the conductor who did eventually lead the premiere, Kirill Kondrashin, came under immense pressure to drop out right up to the last moment. A planned televising of the concert was cancelled on the day of the performance, and the government box at the theatre was conspicuously empty while the rest of the theatre was packed-out.

At the premiere itself the audience broke protocol by breaking out into applause and cheering after the end of the first movement set to the 'Babi Yar' poem. Only the pleadings of Kondrashin persuaded the audience to stop. At the end of the piece, following a few moments of hushed silence, the audience once again exploded in applause and cries of 'Bravo'. Yet the next day's edition of *Pravda* noted the performance in a single sentence buried among other minor notices. Apart from a couple more performances in the provinces the following year, the symphony ceased to be performed in the USSR, and was effectively banned.

There are not many who in middle age, after many years in the wilderness, would have jeopardised their careers by so openly challenging the Soviet dictatorship in the way Shostakovich did in his *Thirteenth Symphony*. As we have seen this was not the first time Shostakovich had acted with such bravery, and this symphony was perhaps the most openly dissident work he was to produce. Sadly, it was also effectively his last public act of resistance to the Soviet regime.

IN OCTOBER 1964, IN A 'palace coup', Khrushchev was deposed and replaced by the far more conservative figure of Leonid Brezhnev. In retrospect, the period of Brezhnev's rule, which ended with his death in 1982, was one of economic stagnation which in turn signalled the decay of the Stalinist political system. Eventually the USSR would collapse under the weight of its inability to match the West economically and from the increasing resistance towards its rule both internally and in its satellite states in Eastern Europe.

In a final, tragic turn in his intimate relationship with the tortured history of the USSR, Shostakovich would experience a painful physical and spiritual decay, paralleling that of Soviet society generally, from the early 1960s until his death in 1975. He had experienced the first symptoms of a mysterious illness in 1958 while performing in France. He had begun to experience a gradual weakening in the right side of his body, the cause of which for many years remained unexplained despite treatment from the best doctors available. One of the effects of the illness was the loss of his ability to play the piano. Although he had concentrated on his career as a composer, he had continued throughout the years to give concerts. As late as 1958 he was making recordings of his own piano concertos. To lose the ability to play must have been devastating for one of his talent. His life increasingly became a round of hospital admissions and tests alongside his increasing paralysis. His third wife, Irina, became as much his full-time carer as his companion.

In 1966 the Brezhenev regime went on the offensive against the intelligentsia. The writers Yuli Daniel and Andrei Sinyavsky were convicted in a closed trial of 'anti-Soviet' activities, and were given long sentences of hard labour. Outrage over this trial led directly to a growing movement of dissident artists and intellectuals in the USSR. Having on many occasions demonstrated courage in speaking his mind, or defending colleagues in trouble with the authorities, Shostakovich disgraced himself by allowing his name to be put to a letter to *Pravda* denouncing one of the most prominent dissidents, Andrei Sakharov. In response to this, Shostakovich's friend the theatre director Yuri Lyubimov refused to shake his hand at a concert. Shostakovich's name was repeatedly attached to other official letters and statements, although family and close friends have claimed that this was often done without his prior knowledge. Nevertheless, given his enormous stature both within the USSR and internationally, Shostakovich could and should have spoken up in defence of the dissident movement, particularly as he himself had been a brave dissident from the 1930s onwards. Instead he came to be seen by many as part of a conservative establishment. No doubt he had been broken by years of persecution, and now debilitating ill health. This is evident in his advice to Rostropovich shortly before the latter's expulsion from the USSR for defending Solzhenitsyn:

Don't waste your efforts. Work, play. You're living here, in this country, and you must see everything as it really is. Don't create illusions. There's no other life. There can't be any. Just be thankful that you're still allowed to breathe.[1]

Death

Spiritual, or moral, decay was evidenced in the disappearance of any protest or indeed any commentary at all on political and social life in his music. The confluence of his own degenerating physical condition and the degeneration of the society with which he was so intimately bound up only contributed to the increasingly despairing mood of his work. Death replaced war, oppression and revolution as the defining theme in his music from the *Seven Songs on Poems by Alexander Blok* (1967), his last four string quartets and the final two symphonies through to one of his last compositions, the *Suite on Verses by Michelangelo Buonarrotti* (1974). *The Fourteenth Symphony* (1969) in particular has been described as an 'anti-requiem', because it describes not merely death, but the 'endless agonies of the dying and empathy for all those being killed, spiritually mortified'.[2] So bleak is this music that at a private first performance of the symphony Solzhenitsyn criticised it for its lack of 'light' in the finale. In a macabre twist Pavel Apostolov, one of Shostakovich's leading persecutors in the Composers' Union in 1948, had a heart attack during this same closed performance, from which he died a month later.

There was certainly no diminution in the musical quality of his later work. On the contrary, the last decade of his life witnessed, as with Beethoven, a 'late style' which plumbed new emotional depths. Again like Beethoven,

Shostakovich's 'late style' saw the composer adopt a style perhaps even more adventurous than in his youth. In the *Fourteenth Symphony*, and the *Thirteenth* (1970) and *Fifteenth* (1974) string quartets, for example, he makes extensive use of Schoenberg's 'serialist' method. To the end of his life Shostakovich remained refreshingly unconcerned about the barriers between different kinds of music. Defending his use of serialism, he said, 'But one finds examples of it in Mozart's music'.[3] And on a trip to London in the early 1970s he deflated some of his more snobbish hosts by declaring his enjoyment of a performance of *Jesus Christ Superstar*. In his final symphony, the *Fifteenth*, he begins with what seems to be a throwback to his early vivaciousness, and bizarrely begins to quote the galloping theme from Rossini's *Overture to William Tell*. By the end of the symphony the mood has descended into tragedy, with quotations from Wagner's *Ring of the Nibelung*. The fact that he brazenly chooses to quote from both Rossini and Wagner in the same piece also demonstrates even at the end of his life Shostakovich's disavowal of the popular/high art dichotomy.

In the year before his death the last remaining buried work from his youth was resurrected. For the first time since 1930 *The Nose* was staged in the USSR. The impetus came from a small artistic company including students. Shostakovich attended most of the rehearsals, and even suggested a Brechtian idea that when the main character decries the absurdity of the concept of a nose leaving a face, the actor playing him should walk up to Shostakovich sitting in the audience and admonish him. Luckily documentary footage survives of the rehearsals for *The Nose*, and they show a clearly very ill Shostakovich nevertheless revelling in what until then had been a lost child of his youth. The revival of *The Nose* seemed to inspire him to work on a long-planned project of composing an opera based on Chekhov's *The Black Monk*. Sadly, he would die before completing it.

Along with the degenerative condition, finally diagnosed as motor neurone disease, Shostakovich suffered a series of heart attacks in the late 1960s and early 1970s. In 1973 it was also discovered that he was suffering from lung cancer. Finally after much suffering and just a few days after completing his haunting final work, the *Sonata for Viola and Piano*, on 9 August 1975 he died at the age of 68.

IN THE DAYS FOLLOWING his death the Soviet press hailed Shostakovich as a "loyal son of the Soviet Union" and the official obituary was signed by, among others, Brezhnev. In the West this view of Shostakovich's politics was supported with a front page obituary in the *Times,* referring to Shostakovich as 'a committed believer in communism and Soviet power'.

However, four years after Shostakovich's death *Testimony* was published. This book, purporting to be his memoirs as dictated to the journalist Solomon Volkov, exploded the image of Shostakovich as a true believer in Communism and the Soviet system. Filled with bitterness about his treatment at the hands of the Soviet dictatorship, *Testimony* was lauded in the West as a true portrait of Communism's oppression of the creative spirit. In the USSR, perhaps unsurprisingly, the book was described as a fraud. Family, friends and students were united in describing Volkov as someone who had, at best, wilfully misinterpreted Shostakovich's words, and at worst simply made much of the 'testimony' up. Partly in response to this book, a collection of articles published by the British Communist Party publishing house disgracefully endorsed the 1936 attacks on Shostakovich as 'clear-sightedness'.[1] The chapter on his symphonies omits any discussion of his *Thirteenth Symphony*, and describes the *Second Symphony* as a Socialist Realist piece, solely on the basis that it celebrates the October revolution, when in fact it was denounced by Stalinist hacks at the time for its modernism.[2]

In the 30 years since the publication of *Testimony* much ink has been spilt arguing over its authenticity, and in attempts to identify Shostakovich's true political beliefs.[3]

Dozens of biographies, reminiscences, musicological analyses, conferences, published symposia and academic articles have been dedicated to this debate, sometimes referred to as 'The Shostakovich Wars'. At times the discussion has been reduced to childish levels with authors describing each other as 'stupid' and 'ignorant'. At other times the issue of Shostakovich's political beliefs, and the true meaning of his music, has led to accusations being made of participants in the debate as KGB agents or of being akin to Holocaust deniers. The battle over Shostakovich's legacy has been brutal and relentless.

Why should Shostakovich be the focus of such an angry debate? One reason could be that the timing of *Testimony's* publication in 1979 coincided with a sharpening of Cold War tensions following the USSR's invasion of Afghanistan, and shortly afterwards by the ascendance of the hawkish administration of Ronald Reagan. But this fails to explain why the arguments should have continued, and indeed intensified, in the decades that have followed the collapse of the USSR and the end of the Cold War.

My own view is that Shostakovich's life and music sit uncomfortably with both the established narrative of the history of the USSR, and the mainstream view of what music, particularly classical music, should be. As I have tried to show in this book, Shostakovich's greatness is inseparable from the revolution of 1917. Not only did he celebrate the revolution explicitly in several early works of the highest quality, but he seemed to express in several later works the belief that Stalinism was not the continuation, but the betrayal of the revolution. And musically he resisted the divide between classical and popular music, thus forcing musicologists and other guardians of 'high' art to dismiss his non-classical works as mere hackwork produced under duress, which is demonstrably untrue in many of his compositions. Shostakovich did not look down on his audience, he did not patronise us with 'accessibility', nor did he attempt to shock us with 'the truth'. Instead, in one masterpiece after another, he attempted to engage us in the defining themes of our age: revolution, war, oppression; occasionally giving us hope, more often despair, but consistently reaching out to a mass audience at the highest artistic level. In this aspect of his life and work, he carried the sprit of the October revolution throughout his life, and has bequeathed it

to us in his music.

Introduction

1   Leon Trotsky, *History of the Russian revolution* (Pluto 1997), p1192-3

2   Andrei Platonov quoted in Levon Kakobian, 'A Perspective on Soviet Musical Culture' in Malcolm Hamrick Brown (ed) *A Shostakovich Casebook* (Indiana University, 2004) p219

3   Robert Stradling, 'Shostakovich and the Soviet System, 1925-1975' in Christopher Norris (ed.) *Shostakovich: The Man and his Music* (Lawrence and Wishart, 1982) p190

4   Gerald McBurney, 'Whose Shostakovich?' in Malcolm Hamrick Brown (ed), op cit, p283

5   Article in *The Guardian*, 13 February 1998, quoted in 'Introduction', Rosamund Bartlett (ed) *Shostakovich in Context*, (Oxford University, 2000) pxiv

Chapter 1: Classical Music and revolution

1   The following is excerpted from an extended discussion of this relationship in Simon Behrman, 'From Revolution to Irrelevance: How classical Music Lost its Audience' in *International Socialism 121* (winter 2009)

2   One of the first professional orchestras to emerge was the Leipzig Gewandhaus that still exists today as one of Europe's leading orchestras. It began life in 1743 with funds supplied by sixteen local businessmen. Another orchestra set up in Halle the same year was financed through the local Masonic Lodge. See

Henry Raynor, *A Social History of Music: From the Middle Ages to Beethoven* (Barrie and Jenkins, 1972), p314-316.

3   Often described as expressing a set of natural and universal musical laws, this is in fact an arbitrary ordering of pitches into whole-tones and semi-tones (respectively the white and black keys on a piano). The multitude of quartertones, and microtones that lie in between these notes are excluded from this scale. In addition, this scale is unique to Western Europe during a specific period. Thus to describe classical tonality as 'natural' and 'atonality' as unnatural involves a breathtaking Euro-centrism. One of the liberatory aspects of modernist music in the 20th century is the rediscovery and use of these 'hidden' pitches.

4   See, for an excellent study of the development of this cult, Esteban Buch, *Beethoven's Ninth: A Political History* (Chicago University, 2004)

Chapter 2: Child of the revolution

1   Until February 1918 Russia still used the old Julian calendar, which was 13 days behind the modern Gregorian calendar. All dates given in brackets refer to the Gregorian calendar.

2   *Testimony* appeared in 1979, four years after Shostakovich's death, purporting to be his memoirs. The authenticity of *Testimony* has been contested ever since. See the Epilogue of this book for further discussion.

3   Elizabeth Wilson, *Shostakovich: A Life Remembered* (Faber, 2006) p376

4   Victor Serge, *Year One of the Russian revolution* (Pluto, 1991)

Chapter 3: The Golden Age

1   Elizabeth Wilson, op cit, p28

2   'Persimfans' was the abbreviation for Perviy Simfonicheskiy Ansambl' bez Dirizhyora (First Conductorless Symphony Ensemble)

3   Gerald MacBurney, op cit, p292

4   Quoted in Alex Ross, *The Rest is Noise: Listening to the Twentieth century* (Harper Perennial, 2009), p239

5   Henry Raynor, op cit, p355

6   Pauline Fairclough, *A Soviet Credo: Shostakovich's Fourth Symphony* (Ashgate, 2006), p xxviii

7   See, for example, David Schroeder, *Cinema's Illusions, Opera's Allure* (Continuum, 2003); Jeremy Tambling, *Opera, Ideology and Film* (Palgrave Macmillan, 1987). Thanks to Louis Bayman for these references.

Chapter 4: Composing a revolution

1   Theodor W Adorno, *Philosophy of New Music* (University of Minnesota, 2006)

2   Elizabeth Wilson, op cit, p12

3   Interview in booklet accompanying recording of the complete symphonies conducted by Rostropovich issued by Teldec (0630-17046-2)

4   Quoted in Pauline Fairclough, op cit, p5

5   Elizabeth Wilson, op cit, p353

6   Quoted in booklet accompanying recording of *Second Symphony*, USSR Ministry of Culture Orchestra, conducted by Gennadi Rozhdestvensky, issued by Melodiya (OCD 258)

7   Arnold Schoenberg, 'New Music, Outmoded Music, Style and Idea' in Leonard Stein (ed), *Style and Idea* (Berkeley, 1984), p124

Chapter 5: The end of the party

1   For a detailed analysis of this process see Tony Cliff, *State Capitalism in Russia* (Bookmarks, 1988)

2   Pauline Fairclough, op cit, p14

3   Ibid, p21

4   Melodiya recording of *Second Symphony*, op cit

5   Quoted in Geoffrey Norris, 'The Operas' in Christopher Norris (ed), op cit, p108

6   Shostakovich in the introduction to the libretto of the opera, quoted in Robert Stradling, op cit, p212

7   Elizabeth Wilson, op cit, p134

8   Pauline Fairclough, op cit, p22

Chapter 6: Terror and resistance

1   *Story of a Friendship: The Letters of Dmitri Shostakovich to Isaak Glikman 1941-1975* (Faber, 2001), p194

2   Pauline Fairclough, op cit, p. xxi, (footnote)

3   Laurel Fay, *Shostakovich: A Life* (Oxford University, 2000), p96

4   Pauline Fairclough, op cit, p234-5

5   Ibid, p237

6   Inna Barsova, 'Between "Social Demands" and the 'Music of Grand Passions': The Years 1934-1937 in the Life of Dimitry Shostakovich' in Rosamund Bartlett (ed), op cit, p94

7   Elizabeth Wilson, op cit, p157

8   Ibid, p152

9   M.M. Bakhtin, *The Dialogical Imagination: Four Essays* (University of Texas, 1981)

10 For further discussion on Bakhtin and the application of his ideas to music, see Pauline Fairclough, op cit, p63-66

11 Theodor W Adorno, op cit; Theodor W. Adorno, 'The Radio Symphony', 'On the Fetish-Character in Music and the Regression of Listening' and 'On the Social Situation of Music' in Richard Leppert (ed) *Essays on Music* (University of California, 2002). It is telling that in his essay (also found in this collection) 'The Dialectical Composer', the relationship described is solely that of the composer to musical tradition; the audience, apparently, plays no part in this dynamic process.

12 Richard Taruskin quoted in Paul Mitchinson 'The Shostakovich Variations', in Malcolm Hamrick Brown (ed), op cit, p318

Chapter 7: From war hero to pariah

1   Elizabeth Wilson, op cit, p335

Chapter 8: The Thaw

1   *Memories of Shostakovich: Interviews with the composer's children by the Revd Michael Ardov*, (Short Books, 2004). p92

2   This musical cryptogram was inspired by Johann Sebastian Bach's frequent use of the same device in his music using the letters

B-A-C-H. The DSCH motif is made up of the notes D-E flat-C-B, which in German notation is D-Es-C-H. Further, in German Shostakovich's name is transliterated from the Cyrillic alphabet as Schostakowitsch. Hence D-Es-C-H = Dmitri [E]sCHostakowitsch.

3   Elizabeth Wilson, op cit, p361

4   Letter of 19 July 1960, in *Story of a Friendship*, op cit, p90-91

5   Irina Nikolskaya, 'Shostakovich Remembered: Interviews with His Soviet Colleagues', in Malcolm Hamrick Brown (ed), op cit, p168

6   Elizabeth Wilson, op cit, p348

7   For further discussion of the post-war avant-garde, see Simon Behrman, op cit

8   Elizabeth Wilson, op cit, p414

Chapter 9: Decay

1   Elizabeth Wilson, Ibid, p487

2   Henry Orlov, op cit, p212

3   Elizabeth Wilson, op cit, p461

Epilogue: 'The Shostakovich Wars'

1   Christopher Norris, 'Shostakovich: politics and musical language' in Christopher Norris (ed), op cit, p181

2   Robert Dearling, 'The First Twelve Symphonies' ibid, p51

3   In two articles, one written in 1980 and the second in 2002, Laurel Fay has comprehensively, and in great detail, demolished the authenticity of *Testimony*. See Laurel Fay, 'Shostakovich versus Volkov: Whose Testimony?' and 'Volkov's Testimony Reconsidered' in Malcolm Hamrick Brown (ed), op cit. At best, *Testimony* represents a collection of anecdotes which circulated among Shostakovich's friends, along with stories which had previously appeared in published interviews and articles by Shostakovich over the years. But too much of the material, particularly the revisionist descriptions of the political meanings in his own works, is not corroborated anywhere else. The difficulty in knowing which bits are genuine if second-hand bits of information, and which are made up, makes the book as a whole, in my opinion, worthless.

Further reading

ON SHOSTAKOVICH

Christopher Norris (ed) *Shostakovich: The Man and his Music* (Lawrence and Wishart, 1982)

Elizabeth Wilson, *Shostakovich: A Life Remembered* (Faber, 2006)

Laurel Fay, *Shostakovich: A Life* (Oxford University, 2000)

Malcolm Hamrick Brown (ed), *A Shostakovich Casebook*, (Indiana University, 2004)

Memories of Shostakovich: Interviews with the Composer's Children by the Revd Michael Ardov, (Short Books, 2004)

Pauline Fairclough, *A Soviet Credo: Shostakovich's Fourth Symphony* (Ashgate, 2006)

Rosamund Bartlett (ed)) *Shostakovich in Context*, (Oxford University, 2000)

Story of a Friendship: The Letters of Dmitri Shostakovich to Isaak Glikman 1941-1975 (Faber, 2001)

ON CLASSICAL MUSIC

Albrecht Betz, *Hanns Eisler: Political Musician* (Cambridge University, 1982)

Alex Ross, *The Rest is Noise: Listening to the Twentieth century* (Harper Perennial, 2009)

Anthony Arblaster, *Viva la Liberta!: Politics in Opera* (Verso, 1992)

Daniel Barenboim and Edward W Said, *Parallels and Paradoxes: Explorations in Music and Society* (Bloomsbury, 2003)

115

Edward W Said, *Musical Elaborations* (Vintage, 1991)

Esteban Buch, *Beethoven's Ninth: A Political History,* (Chicago University, 2004)

Guy Rickards, *Hindemith, Hartmann and Henze* (Phaidon, 1995)

Hanns Eisler, *A Rebel in Music: Selected Writings* (Kahn and Averill, 1999)

Hans Werner Henze, *Bohemian Fifths: An Autobiography* (Faber, 1998)

Henry Raynor, *A Social History of Music: From the Middle Ages to Beethoven* (Barrie and Jenkins, 1972)

Joseph Horowitz, *Classical Music in America: A History of its Rise and Fall* (Norton, 2005)

Joseph Horowitz, *Understanding Toscanini* (Faber, 1987)

Leonard Bernstein, *The Infinite Variety of Music* (Amadeus, 2007)

Leonard Bernstein, *The Joy of Music* (Amadeus, 2004)

Paul McGarr, *Mozart: Overture to revolution* (Redwords, 2001)

Simon Behrman, 'From Revolution to Irrelevance: How Classical Music Lost its Audience' in *International Socialism 121* (Winter 2009)

Theodor W Adorno, *Essays on Music* (University of California, 2002)

On Marxism and art in general

Henri Arvon, *Marxist Esthetics* (Cornell University, 1973)

Leon Trotsky, *Literature and revolution* (Haymarket, 2009)

Berel Lang and Forrest Williams (eds) *Marxism and Art: Writings in Aesthetics and Criticism,* (David McKay, 1972)

Theodor Adorno, Walter Benjamin, Ernst Bloch, Bertolt Brecht and George Lukacs, *Aesthetics and Politics* (Verso, 1980)

On the Russian revolution

John Reed, *Ten Days That Shook the World* (Penguin, 2007)

Leon Trotsky, *History of the Russian revolution* (Pluto, 1997)

Leon Trotsky, *The revolution Betrayed* (Dover, 2004)

Moshe Lewin, *Lenin's Last Struggle* (University of Michigan, 2005)

Tony Cliff, *State Capitalism in Russia* (Bookmarks, 1988)

Victor Serge, *From Lenin to Stalin* (Pathfinder, 1973)

Victor Serge, *Year One of the Russian revolution* (Pluto, 1991)

Further listening

WORKS BY SHOSTAKOVICH

What follows is by no means an exhaustive list of Shostakovich's works. There are after all well over 150 of them and indeed many pieces are of a low standard, eg many of the propaganda works that he was forced to write over the years. But there are also many fine pieces for which there is simply no space. Instead, listed, below are all the pieces discussed in the book and a few others, along with some recommended recordings. In brackets next to each piece are numbers referring to the pages in this book where it is referred to. Please bear in mind that the recommendations are highly subjective, and do not purport to be 'definitive' recordings – such things are a logical impossibility which only exist in the world of marketing. But hopefully, they will help those readers new to Shostakovich's music to begin to negotiate their way through the hundreds of available recordings of his works.

Complete Symphonies:
Various orchestras, Conducted by Mstislav Rostropovich (Teldec)

Complete Symphonies:
Moscow Philharmonic Orchestra, Conducted by Kyrill Kondrashin (Melodiya)

First Symphony (1925) – Philadelphia Orchestra, Conducted by Eugene Ormandy. (Sony Classical) This recording also includes a wonderful selection of some of Shostakovich's jazz and light music compositions conducted by Andre Kostelanetz.

Second Symphony 'October' (1927) – USSR Ministry of Culture Symphony

Orchestra, Conducted by Gennadi Rozhdestvensky (Olympia) Also includes the *Fifteenth Symphony* and the '*The Bedbug*' *Suite* (1929)

Fourth Symphony (1936) – Philharmonia Orchestra, Conducted by Gennadi Rozhdestvensky (BBC Legends). This is a live recording of the first performance of the symphony outside the USSR. It also includes the rarely heard 'Katerina Ismailova' Suite.

Fifth Symphony (1937) – Leningrad Philharmonic, Conducted by Evgeny Mravinsky (Erato). This is a visceral live performance from the 1980s, with the same conductor and orchestra who gave the premiere of this symphony in 1937.

• For an interpretation diametrically opposed to this one try, New York Philharmonic, Conducted by Leonard Bernstein (Sony Classical)

Seventh Symphony 'Leningrad' (1942) – Czech Philharmonic Orchestra, Conducted by Karel Ancerl (Supraphon)

•NBC Symphony Orchestra, Conducted by Arturo Toscanini (RCA Victor, Vol. 22 of the Arturo Toscanini Collection). This is a recording of the historic premiere performance outside the USSR, broadcast live across the USA in 1942.

Eighth Symphony (1943) – Leningrad Philharmonic Orchestra, Conducted by Evgeny Mravinsky (Philips)

Tenth Symphony (1953) – USSR Ministry of Culture Symphony Orchestra, Conducted by Gennadi Rozhdestvensky (Olympia). This CD also includes music Shostakovich composed for the scandalously avant-garde 1932 production of *Hamlet* staged by Nikolai Akimov.

Eleventh Symphony 'The Year 1905' (1957) – Leningrad Philharmonic Orchestra, Conducted by Evgeny Mravinsky (Praga)

Thirteenth Symphony 'Babi Yar' (1962) – Moscow Philharmonic Orchestra, Conducted by Kyrill Kondrashin (Russian Disc). This is the live recording of the work's premiere in 1962. It includes the original version of the poems, performed in defiance of the authorities at the time. Although this recording is often hard to find, it is an absolutely electric performance and well worth seeking out.

Fifteenth Symphony (1971) – Kremerata Musica (Deutsche Grammophon). This is a chamber version arranged by Viktor Derevianko with the composer's blessing. It brilliantly captures many of the details, especially in the first movement, which are often lost in full orchestral performances. Few performances are able to convey the strange spectral nature of this work as well as this one does. In addition, this recording includes a short piece by Alfred Schnittke composed in memory of Shostakovich, using the musical monogram DSCH.

• There are three sets of the complete string quartets that I would recommend:

• The Beethoven Quartet (Doremi) were the dedicatees of several of the quartets, and were almost always afforded the honour by Shostakovich of giving the first performances.

• The Fitzwilliam Quartet (Decca) made their recordings under the supervision of the composer shortly before his death.

• However, in my opinion the Borodin Quartet (Melodiya) play with the most feeling, and take the greatest risks in their interpretation. This set also includes the *Piano Quintet* with the Borodins joined by the incomparable pianist Sviatoslav Richter.

Theme & Variations (1922) – London Symphony Orchestra, Conducted by Leon Botstein (Telarc). This recording also includes Gavril Popov's *First Symphony*.

First Piano Sonata (1926) – Konstantin Scherbakov (Naxos) Also includes, *Aphorisms (1927), 24 Preludes (1932)* and *Three Fantastic Dances (1922)*.

The Nose (1928) – Moscow Chamber Theatre, Conducted by Gennadi Rozhdestvensky (Melodiya). The recording of the 1970s revival, overseen by Shostakovich shortly before his death. It also includes the first performance of *The Gamblers*, an unfinished opera, also based on Gogol, composed by Shostakovich in 1942.

The New Babylon (1929) – Berlin Radio Symphony Orchestra, Conducted by James Judd (Capriccio). Also includes the score from the film *Five Days, Five Nights (1960)*

Alone (1930) – Frankfurt Radio Symphony Orchestra, Conducted by Mark Fitz-Gerald (Naxos)

Lady Macbeth of the Mtsensk District (1932) – London Philharmonic Orchestra, Conducted by Mstislav Rostropovich, with Galina Vishnevskaya as Katerina Ismailova (EMI Classics)

The Tale of the Priest and his Servant Balda (1933) – USSR Ministry of Culture Orchestra, Conducted by Gennadi Rozhdestvensky (Melodiya) This two-CD set simply titled Orchestral Works includes a treasure trove of other rarely heard *gems by Shostakovich.*

Concerto for Piano, Trumpet and Strings (1933) – Dmitri Shostakovich, Orchestre National de la Radiodiffusion Francaise, Conducted by Andre Cluytens (EMI Classics). A chance to hear the brilliance of Shostakovich as a pianist in his own works. This also includes recordings of the *Second Piano Concerto* along with the *Three Fantastic Dances (1922)* and a selection from the *24 Preludes and Fugues (1950)*

Second Piano Trio (1944) – Martha Argerich, Gidon Kremer and Mischa Maisky (Deutsche Grammophon). Also includes *Tchaikovsky's Piano Trio.*

First Violin Concerto (1948) – David Oistrakh, New York Philharmonic, Conducted by Dmitri Mitropoulos (Sony Classical). Also includes Rostropovich and the Philadelphia Orchestra under Eugene Ormandy performing the *First Cello Concerto* (1959).

The two-volume set *The Orchestral Songs* – Gothenburg Symphony Orchestra, Conducted by Neeme Järvi (Deutsche Grammophon). These include excellent recordings of *From Jewish Folk Poetry* (1948) and the *Suite on Verses by Michelangelo Buonarrotti (1974)*

Anti-Formalist Rayok (1948) – The world premiere recording, conducted by Mstislav Rostropovich (Erato) if you can find it. The only current readily available recording appears to be by the Moscow Virtuosi, Conducted by Vladimir Spivikov (Capriccio)

Twenty Four Preludes and Fugues (1950) – Tatiana Nikolaeva (Melodiya). The best of several recordings made by the dedicatee of this work.

The Gadfly (1955) – BBC Philharmonic Orchestra, Conducted by Vassily Sinaisky (Chandos). This also includes two scores from the 1930s, *The Golden Mountains* and *Volochayev Days*.

The Execution of Stepan Razin (1964) – Varna Philharmonic Orchestra, Conducted by Andre Andreev (Koch International Classics). This CD also includes a curiosity, *Oratorio Pathetique,* a setting of poems by Vladimir Mayakovsky composed by Georgy Sviridov, one of Shostakovich's pupils.

Seven Songs on Poems by Alexander Blok (1967) – Galina Vishnevskaya, David Oistrakh, Mstislav Rostropovich, Moishei Vainberg (Melodiya). This is a classic recording including some of the greatest names in Soviet musical life. This live performance also includes *Songs and Dances of Death* by Mussorgsky and orchestrated by Shostakovich.

King Lear (1970) – Rundfunk Symphonie Orchester Berlin, Conducted by Michail Jurowski (Capriccio). Also includes Shostakovich's score for a stage production in the late 1930s.

Sonata for Viola and Piano (1975) – Yuri Bashmet and Sviatoslav Richter (Regis) Also includes recordings of both of Shostakovich's *Violin Sonatas*.

The Jazz Album – Royal Concertgebouw Orchestra, Conducted by Riccardo Chailly (Decca). An excellent collection of some of Shostakovich's jazz-inspired works.

Below are listed works by composers who influenced Shostakovich, were influenced by him and others who were his contemporaries. This list is, again, by no means exhaustive. Rather it is merely intended to guide readers who wish to further explore the musical world, of which Shostakovich was a part. The pieces and recordings suggested have been chosen because of their relevance to Shostakovich, and unavoidably based on my own preferences.

Modest Mussorgsky: Boris Godunov – Boris Christoff, Conservatoire Concert Society Orchestra, Conducted by Andre Cluytens (EMI Classics)

Nicolai Rimsky-Korsakov: Scheherazade – Chicago Symphony Orchestra, Conducted by Fritz Reiner (Living Stereo) Also includes Stravinsky's *Song of the Nightingale.*

Gustav Mahler: Second Symphony "Resurrection" – London Symphony Orchestra, Conducted by Leopold Stokowski (BBC Legends)

• Sixth Symphony – Vienna Philharmonic Orchestra, Conducted by Pierre Boulez (Deutsche Grammophon)

• Seventh Symphony – Berlin Philharmonic, Conducted by Claudio Abbado (Deutsche Grammophon)

Igor Stravinsky: Petrushka and The Rite of Spring – Cleveland Orchestra, Conducted by Pierre Boulez (Deutsche Grammophon)

• Stravinsky conducts Stravinsky – Orchestra della Radiotelevisione della Svizzera Italiana, Conducted by Igor Stravinsky (Ermitage) A live performance of some of his most jazz influenced works.

Alexander Glazunov: Violin Concerto – Jascha Heifetz, RCA Victor Symphony Orchestra, Conducted by Walter Hendl (RCA) Also includes violin concertos by Sibelius and Prokofiev.

Alban Berg: Wozzeck – Stockholm Royal Opera, Conducted by Leif Segerstam (Naxos)

Arnold Schoenberg: Piano Concerto – Mitsuko Uchida, Cleveland Orchestra, Conducted by Pierre Boulez (Philips) Also includes various solo piano pieces by Schoenberg and his students Anton Webern and Alban Berg.

Ralph Vaughan-Williams: Fourth Symphony – New Philharmonia Orchestra, Conducted by Adrian Boult (EMI Classics) Also includes the Sixth Symphony.

Kurt Weill: The Threepenny Opera – RIAS Berlin Sinfonietta, Conducted by John Mauceri (Decca)

Hanns Eisler: Song Collection – Various artists (Berlin Classics)

Paul Hindemith: Kammermusik – Royal Concertgebouw Orchestra, Conducted by Riccardo Chailly (Decca)

Arseni Avraamov: Symphony of Sirens (ReR Megacorp) This also includes an incredible array of recordings of other experimental musical compositions, poetry and political speeches from the 'Golden Age' of the 1920s. It can only be bought via the website www.rermegacorp.com

• Music of the First October Years – Various artists (Melodiya) – This CD includes works by Gavril Popov, Alexander Mosolov, Alexei Zhivotov and Nikolai Myaskovsky.

Sergei Prokofiev: Alexander Nevsky – St. Petersburg Philharmonic Orchestra, Conducted by Yuri Temirkanov (RCA)

• Fifth Symphony, Scythian Suite – London Symphony Orchestra/Minneapolis Symphony, Conducted by Antal Dorati (Mercury Living Presence)

Aram Khachaturian: Suites from Spartacus and Gayaneh – Vienna Philharmonic Orchestra, Conducted by Aram Khachaturian (London) Also includes excerpts from Romeo and Juliet by Prokofiev.

Benjamin Britten: War Requiem – London Symphony Orchestra, Conducted by Benjamin Britten (Decca)

Sofia Gubaidulina: Stimmen...Verstummen – Stockholm Philharmonic Orchestra, Conducted by Gennadi Rozhdestvensky (Chandos)

Alfred Schnittke: First Concerto Grosso – Chamber Orchestra of Europe, Conducted by Heinrich Schiff (Deutsche Grammophon) Also includes works by Witold Lutoslawski and Gyorgy Ligeti.

Edison Denisov: Concerto for Alto Saxophone and other pieces – Claude Delangle, BBC National Orchestra of Wales, Conducted by Tadaaki Otaka (BIS)

Boris Tishchenko: Fifth Symphony – USSR Ministry of Culture Symphony Orchestra, Conducted by Gennadi Rozhdestvensky (Olympia)

Galina Ustvolskaya: Octet, Composition No. 3, Fifth Symphony – London Musici, Conducted by Mark Stephenson (Conifer) Also includes a performance of Shostakovich's Piano Quintet.

This book is in the series *Revolutionary Portraits* from Redwords. The unifying theme in this eclectic collection is the relationship between individual artists and larger historical forces, how each influences and shapes the other. All of the books in the series aim to lead us back to these works of art and music with new eyes and ears, and a deeper understanding of how art can raise the human spirit.

Redwords is a publishing collective specialising in art, history and literature from a socialist perspective.

Others:
Mozart
Rembrandt
Diego Rivera
John Coltrane
William Blake
William Shakespeare
William Morris
Frank SInatra

Forthcoming:
Charlie Chaplin
Alexander Rodchenko
Charlie Parker
Bob Dylan

www.redwords.org.uk